I Can't Believe I Did That!

I Can't Believe I Did That!

Instinctive Behavior In Humans

David L. Carlson

To order additional copies of this book, contact:
Xlibris Corporation
1-888-795-4274
www.Xlibris.com
Orders@Xlibris.com
44371

CONTENTS

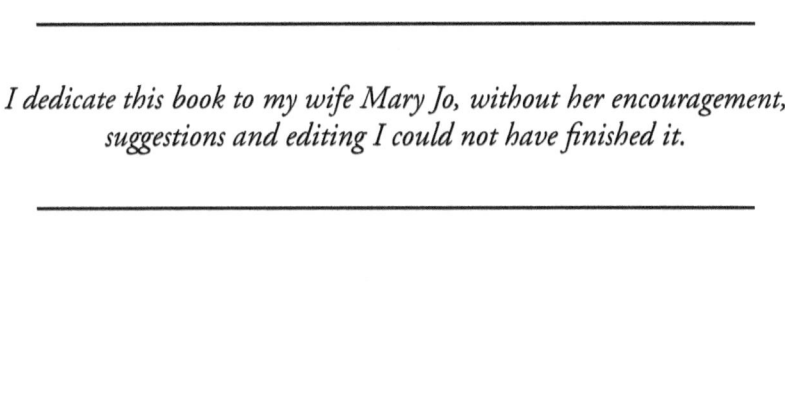

I dedicate this book to my wife Mary Jo, without her encouragement, suggestions and editing I could not have finished it.

PROLOGUE

This is not intended to be a scientific journal. There is no bibliography of source material. In fact, there is no new scientific information here at all. I have merely drawn from many volumes of already established data in an attempt to get a better understanding of human behavior. Anything written here can be easily verified by anyone with a little curiosity about the world of science and the behavior of humans.

Nothing in this writing in any way denies the existence of God or suggests or even implies anything contrary to a belief in God. The whole point is to find some plausible and understandable reasons to explain why we humans engage in the universal responses and actions that have been so prominent throughout the history of mankind.

INTRODUCTION

Why do we behave as we do? There are so many obvious differences among individuals and yet we all share some very basic traits. For instance, we are all very competitive, but why? What is it that drives us to get ahead, to be better at something, anything, than someone else? From global warfare down to sibling rivalry we all compete on a variety of levels every day.

Almost without exception we insist that our territory, our culture, our language, our religion, our way of life in general is the best. All over the world, people feel the same way. No matter what territory we claim as ours, no matter how different our way of life is from all the others, we feel that ours is best. In fact, it's not just the best, it is literally worth fighting and dying for. It is worth killing other human beings for.

It appears that it is not possible for the majority of us to quit fighting, get along, cooperate, and work together in peace and harmony for the good of everyone. Some people have actually tried this concept but it only works in small groups for the short term. Sooner or later, there is dissension and the group falls apart. This is obviously normal behavior since it happens in any group regardless of their philosophy. That's why we tend to break up into smaller groups. We want to do things our way and keep things the way we believe they should be. We ask ourselves, "Why can't those other people see that our way is best?"

So why has the human species always functioned this way? Ask any number of people this question and they will probably shrug and say, "It's the way we are. It's human nature." But what is "human nature?" Where did it come from? Why do we have it? It can't be the collective result of literally trillions of independent decisions. It must be something inherent, something deep, basic and primal that is common to all humans.

Those of us who live in one of the developed countries of the world actually have all these answers, and many more, readily available. Advances in scientific research in biology, physiology, anthropology and other related fields have led to amazing discoveries and accomplishments such as the mapping of the human genome and DNA testing, giving us some insights into what we are all made of.

Most of us are so busy just coping with life in general, we may not have the time or energy or even the interest to delve into the science of human behavior. But for those with even a little curiosity about basic human similarities and tendencies, the answers are out there if we choose to discover them.

Modern technology is literally astounding. Advances in areas such as communications, computers, medicine and space travel, just to name a few, are all based on laws of physics and chemistry painstakingly worked out, refined and proven by generations of scientists. All of these advances that we take for granted every day are the result of progressive scientific discoveries. How can we reasonably accept all of these amazing inventions and conveniences made possible by science and reject one of it's crowning achievements; the concept of evolution?

Evolution is no longer just a theory. It is a proven fact. Even if we disregard the vast amount of evidence in the fossil record, all one has to do is look at what humans have achieved by selective breeding of domestic animals in just a few centuries. How many specialized breeds of dogs, horses and cattle exist now because humans restricted mating to only those with certain desirable qualities?

Qualities and traits such as appearance, size, shape, strength, speed and temperament were selected for and refined in the span of a few hundred years. Think of the differences between Dachshunds, Saint Bernards, Toy Poodles, and Great Danes. They are all descendants of early wolves that were tamed by humans thousands of years ago.

This practice of "animal husbandry" was well known and well documented by the time Charles Darwin gathered his scientific evidence and published his findings. During his meticulous study of birds and other animals, he correctly reasoned that what humans can accomplish in a few hundred years, natural processes would do in a few hundred thousand years and after a few hundred million years the possibilities would be virtually unlimited. Since Darwin's time, advances in fields such as molecular biology, genetics, physiology, paleontology, etc. have overwhelmingly proved his theory.

The vast majority of the population of the world is not aware of this evidence and even some who are aware of it reject it because they feel it goes against religious doctrine. But religious doctrine has changed considerably over the years. For instance, just a few hundred years ago, the earth was thought to be the center of the universe and all celestial bodies revolved around it. Early astronomers who contradicted this concept were forced to recant by the churches or face excommunication, torture or death. As late as 200 years ago some churches and cultures still sanctioned torturing and burning women who were thought to be witches.

The two previous examples show how religious and cultural teachings have changed with time. Changes such as these are literally profound because they prove that some doctrine and teachings that were once accepted as God's will did not come from God at all, but were actually originated by people who may have been convinced that they were speaking for God, but were obviously mistaken.

How can we determine what is true and what is false? The only ideas and concepts we can be sure of are the ones that can be proven. We simply cannot believe everything we are told by people in positions of leadership. Anyone can say anything such as "the world is flat" or "the moon is made of green cheese" but that does not make it true no matter who says it. Leaders in any area or profession can be just as wrong as the rest of us. We must base our beliefs on proven facts.

Science is the only self-correcting discipline we have. Each new theory is met with a healthy skepticism and numerous independent experiments are conducted to prove or disprove it. Only those theories that survive this rigid process are accepted as fact.

Changes in church and cultural doctrine may be slow but most cultures and nearly all major religions have amended their teachings to agree with facts established by science. Some of us who are aware of the evidence supporting evolution, and still reject it, may be unwilling to accept the fact that humans have a kinship with other species. Others may simply believe whatever the church elders or community leaders say. But we all know there are many evil, unholy people in positions of authority in all churches as well as business and government.

Shyster evangelists, cult leaders who advocate brainwashing and pedophiles in all walks of life, including the priesthood, are just a few examples of people who are not what they pretend to be. The Ku Klux Klan had many members professing to be devout Christians, including church elders and even some ministers, who terrorized, tortured and murdered innocent humans. Evil people in any profession are perfectly capable of appearing to be genuine believers.

We all want to believe that people in positions of leadership are honest, sensible and wise. We want them to be genuinely concerned about those of us who are affected by their decisions. We tend to trust them if they say what we want to hear or at least something that sounds reasonable and right. When a respected community or church leader is exposed as a fraud, thief, liar or pedophile, we may feel many different emotions ranging from rage to sad acceptance. Some of us feel like gullible saps for being taken in by someone we thought was so trustworthy.

Optimism is a wonderful trait but wishful thinking is just the opposite. Making assumptions and decisions based on wishful thinking can be compared to wearing blinders that allow us to see only that which we want to be true and obscure real evidence and warning signs. With so many different opinions, ideas and concepts in the technological world of today, a healthy skepticism and some requirement of proof are definite assets to forming a realistic outlook.

Eventually, all the major religions and cultures of the world will incorporate evolution into their belief systems and educational processes as the method used by God to create the wonderful diversity of life on earth. If you don't think so, ask yourself, "How many religions and cultures still maintain that the earth is the center of the universe?"

Just a little knowledge of evolution can explain so much about human behavior and answer questions that have been baffling people for thousands of years.

CHAPTER 1

The Early Earth

The basic history of our planet has been quite accurately deciphered from the geological record; clues in the rocks and fossils from the past. The record is by no means complete. There are still gaps but archeologists and paleontologists are rapidly filling them in. Despite some missing details the big picture of our planet's history and the evolution of life on earth are becoming quite clear.

It has been reliably established that our planet and the rest of our Solar System were formed from cosmic debris about 4.7 billion years ago. The early earth was a very inhospitable place. Initially it consisted mostly of rock and iron that was largely molten due to the intense pressure in the interior and constant bombardment at the surface. There was no air or water. The comets, asteroids and other space debris crashing into the planet added a variety of other elements such as carbon, hydrogen and significant quantities of ice that immediately melted and turned to steam.

During the first billion years the bombardment eventually slowed enough so that parts of the surface cooled. Vast clouds of steam then condensed into pools of liquid water. This set the stage for the beginning of life on earth.

Science has not determined exactly how the first life was formed. We do know that the building blocks necessary for life were present on the early earth. The simplest definition of life is "an entity that is able to reproduce itself." The first life must have been a tiny bit of primitive DNA that somehow gained the ability to reproduce.

The first reproduction was "asexual," meaning that it consisted of the life form being able to split into two identical copies. This method is still found in primitive organisms that exist today such as algae and plankton.

Initially, after the first life came into being, there was abundant raw material for the new organisms to ingest and use as fuel. Existence must have been quite easy, at least in relation to food supply. Eventually, however, the population became too large and competition for food became very important. Thereafter, the cold, hard fact of life known as "Survival of the Fittest" became an integral part of life and has literally been a matter of life and death ever since.

One of the basic principles of evolution is that energy sources such as cosmic and solar radiation occasionally cause very small but permanent changes in DNA at the molecular level of all living organisms. When an organism reproduces this change is faithfully transferred to all ensuing offspring. The majority of these random changes are harmful or even fatal to the offspring who inherit them. Most of the rest are inconsequential, and provide neither advantage nor disadvantage to the inheritor.

Once in a great while, one of these random changes is beneficial to the subsequent offspring. The new characteristic may give them an advantage in the competition for food. Even a small advantage can mean survival and reproduction while other similar organisms, less able to compete, starve or are eaten by predators and leave no descendants. Different habitats favor different mutations so isolation, climate changes and a few hundred thousand generations can result in one species evolving into several others.

At some point during the latter part of the first billion years of our planet's existence the first life became firmly established. Primitive, individual cells slowly became more efficient at reproducing. For the next two and a half billion years the cells proliferated and spread to all the oceans of the earth. With new offspring being exact clones of their parent cell, changes took a lot of time so life remained basically as single-celled organisms.

However, during this time there were some significant advances in differentiation and function. Various strains of bacteria and viruses evolved and the beginnings of symbiotic relationships were established. Initially single cells that grouped together survived better that those that didn't. The green slime that forms in wet areas consists of millions of tiny, primitive organisms and there is evidence that this slime has existed essentially unchanged for billions of years. Obviously, this is a very successful arrangement.

As groups of these primitive organisms proliferated, eventually some groups began living in close proximity to other types. In some cases both groups benefited and soon they became mutually dependent. Eventually, this led to an even closer form of symbiosis where one organism lives inside a larger organism of a different type. Typically both organisms not only benefited from this "host/parasite" arrangement but soon neither could live without the other. All multi-cellular organisms, including humans, are hosts to literally millions of good bacteria, which are absolutely essential to life.

The ultimate form of symbiosis occurred quite early when a tiny bacteria, now known as mitochondria, was somehow incorporated into a larger cell. The mitochondria kept its own DNA separate from the cell DNA but otherwise became an integral part of the host cell. The addition of the mitochondria significantly enhanced the ability of the larger cell to function more efficiently. The combination was so successful that this type of cell is the building block of most life on earth today.

It appears that this whole business of symbiosis could have also led to perhaps the most important evolutionary advancement of all; the original "Sexual Revolution." Somewhere around a billion years ago "sexual" reproduction began. Instead of one cell splitting, now two organisms had to unite in some way so they could contribute half their DNA to form a separate offspring that was not identical to either parent. Combining DNA in this manner, along with mutation, isolation, climate change and eons of time have caused the tremendous variety of life forms that have inhabited the earth during the last billion years.

It took a few million years for this new process to become the dominant method of reproduction but there is now ample fossil evidence that by a half billion years ago there were at least three major groups of large organisms inhabiting the worlds oceans. These groups include the Arthropods or exoskeletons, which were the ancestors of modern insects, the Mollusks, ancestors of shellfish and the Vertebrates, ancestors of all organisms with internal skeletons.

For several reasons the vast majority of the fossil evidence that has already been found or will be found in the future comes from the last 500 million years. Fortunately, this is the period of greatest interest to paleontologists.

Since it takes so many generations for one species to evolve into another, we cannot actually observe it happening in any organisms large enough to see. Even in rapid reproducers such as rabbits, generations take far too long but some microbes can reproduce in hours or even minutes. Since the invention of the electron microscope, we have actually witnessed evolution first-hand by watching microbes.

A typical example is the bacterium, *staphylococcus aureus*, commonly found in hospitals. It causes the dreaded staph infection that has taken the life of many patients who would have otherwise survived. It was nearly eradicated by penicillin in the mid 1940s but because of favorable mutations a very small percentage of these organisms survived and became resistant. The survivors proliferated and in just a few years it was once again a widespread, formidable health threat.

Since that time this microbe has become resistant to several more antibiotics. Even though we still call it by the same name, each new resistant strain is significantly different from earlier strains and each is technically a new species.

The evidence that we can see in larger animals comes from species that have separated relatively recently, perhaps in the last few hundred thousand years. For instance, horses, donkeys and zebras all came from the same ancestor but at some time in the past the ancestral group was split up and the factions were isolated. They are still related closely enough to be similar in appearance and they can even interbreed and produce hybrid offspring but the offspring are infertile.

The most common example is the mule. Mules result from a cross between a horse and a donkey. These two species are genetically far enough apart so that no amount of interbreeding will cause them to merge back into one.

Conversely, all the different breeds of horses from Shetlands to Clydesdales are still part of the same species. They have matching DNA with the same number of genes and chromosomes. An egg from one breed can be fertilized by sperm from any other breed and a fertile offspring will result. With enough interbreeding the specialized types would disappear and eventually all horses would once again look very much alike. The same is true of other species such as dogs, cats, cattle and, of course, humans.

Crossbreeding rarely occurs in the wild but occurs occasionally in zoos. Rare crosses such as the "liger," a mix of lion and tiger, have been found. Among domesticated animals the practice has been used for years to produce beasts of burden such as mules and tasty meat sources such as crossing cattle and buffalo to get "beefalos."

In addition to animal hybrids there are hundreds of plant hybrids that have resulted in significantly improved food crops. Essentially all crops we grow today are hybrids that are of much better quality, have a higher yield per acre and are more disease-resistant and drought-resistant than the original strains.

CHAPTER 2

Religion and Evolution

Scientists agree that the process of evolution occurred after the appearance of the first, tiny life form. The evidence is overwhelming. They do not agree on what actually started that first life. Some say that a natural energy source such as lightning struck certain combinations of existing building-block material and other natural processes did the rest. Some say that God caused it and then oversaw and perhaps even guided the course of evolution. Either way is consistent with the fossil record.

The timing in most religious versions of creation varies considerably from the geological timetable established by scientists. There may be a reasonable explanation for this. Humans are mortal and have relatively short lives here on earth. That may be why we are so impatient and want things done in a hurry. Maybe we are just assuming that God is also in a hurry.

An immortal creator would have always existed and would have no time constraints of any kind. Logically, the colossal job of creating the "Heavens and Earth and all life on Earth" could have been done very slowly over the eons of time reflected in the geological timetable. Perhaps the Old Testament version of the Creation is actually describing the time when God felt that humans were finally ready to receive their souls.

Even the concept of "Intelligent Design" is not ruled out by the evidence. A Creator that caused and guided evolution to produce the wide variety of life on earth would probably not start from scratch to create modern humans. A fully functional, tried and tested existing species, such as one of the early hominids, could have been used with some improvements. Some minor physical changes plus a large brain is all that would be required except for the intangible additions such as a conscience and, of course, a soul.

This is all speculation because it cannot be proven one way or another at the present time. The important thing is that religion and science do not have to be mutually exclusive. In fact, it is imperative that in some way they agree. There must be a reasonable explanation as to why humans are physiologically so similar to animals.

All species are composed of the same carbon-based molecules and we operate with all the same bodily functions. We are born, live for a while and die, just like all other organisms. All living things eat, drink, excrete waste, reproduce and try to survive. Other than external differences such as size and shape, the primary physical feature that sets us apart from other warm-blooded species is the size of our brain.

This all-important organ, the human brain, will be the focus of this quest to get a better understanding of some common human behaviors.

CHAPTER 3

The Brain

The human brain has been meticulously studied for centuries. Its basic physiology and function have been well known for many years and ongoing research constantly adds more details to our knowledge. The brain is not a one-piece organ such as a kidney or liver. It is composed of several distinct sections. The larger parts take up most of the room in our skulls and contain centers for various activities and talents such as decision-making, language, art and music. These larger sections account for the tremendous variety in human thinking, creativity, areas of interest, abilities and intelligence.

The versatility and potential of the human brain is literally awesome. It has enabled us, in the last hundred thousand years to go from just another species struggling to survive to become the dominant species in the world. By utilizing this vast brain capacity we have actually transformed most parts of our planet to better suit our needs.

At the base of the brain there is a small, well-protected and absolutely essential section generally called the "primitive brain stem." All the other parts of the brain are relatively recent evolutionary developments but the stem is the original. This section of the brain is common to all vertebrate species. It controls the basic functions necessary to maintain life, often collectively referred to as the "Instinct of Survival."

These vital instincts are the involuntary functions and responses, such as breathing, digestion, reflexes, sex-drive, hunger and many more. They are automatic and require no thought or decision-making. This remarkable package controls everything that was crucial for a species to compete and flourish in the "Survival of the Fittest" environment. Many humans have lived and done well after major injuries to the larger sections of the brain or even with a section removed, but any injury to the primitive brain stem is normally fatal.

In 1990, a young Florida woman named Terri Schiavo suffered physiological trauma that caused her brain to be deprived of oxygen for at least five minutes. She entered a "persistent vegetative state" from which she would never recover.

In an oxygen deprivation episode, the brain stem is the last section to be deprived and therefore the last to suffer any damage. Mrs. Schiavo's stem continued normal operation so all of the vital signs of her involuntary body functions, e.g. breathing, circulation, digestion, blinking and the rest were positive.

There were high hopes that she would eventually regain consciousness and, with therapy, perhaps resume a normal life. She was kept on a feeding tube for the next fifteen years. After several emotional and highly publicized court battles, the feeding tube was finally removed in 2005. About a week later she was pronounced officially dead.

An autopsy revealed that all sections of her brain, with the exception of the primitive brain stem, had atrophied and there was no indication that they could function at all. Sadly, despite all the available medical technology and the hopes and prayers of the family, there had never been a chance for her recovery. Similar situations can happen to anyone at any time, which is why medical establishments prefer that everyone have written statements available concerning their wishes about life support systems.

The primitive brain stem evolved very early. It had already achieved its basic form and function by the time the first dinosaurs appeared about 250 million years ago. In fact, it is sometimes referred to as the "reptilian brain" because it was the only brain the dinosaurs had. It was obviously enough because they were the dominant life form for about 165 million years.

For at least a half-billion years, this small, primitive organ has been the primary control of all vertebrate species, until humans. As far as we know, humans are the only species able to override any of these primitive instincts. We cannot eliminate the automatic reflexes and urges but we can recognize them for what they are and decide what action to take when we feel them.

Dinosaurs, with all their astounding variations and adaptations, had no ability to reason or to make decisions. No Tyrannosaurus Rex ever decided to ignore hunger and not hunt for food because it decided to go on a diet or that certain prey did not deserve to die and should be spared. Those decisions are higher brain functions that can only be made using other brain sections that did not yet exist. None of the fossils that exist today are there because the creature decided to commit suicide.

Before humans appeared, all species that survived did so almost exclusively on instinct and involuntary response. Since humans also have this primitive brain stem, we have to deal with these same instincts every day. To deal with them effectively, we really need to understand them. Not just some of them but all of them. They are much more prevalent in human behavior than most of us realize. In fact, much of what we refer to as "human nature" is actually instinctive behavior that is common to all species.

A good example of an instinctive reaction that we have all felt hundreds of times is the "startle reflex." We may be sitting around relaxing and feeling safe when all of a sudden, there is a loud noise right behind us. We jerk upright and our heart gets a shot of adrenalin, which prepares us for "fight or flight." This reaction comes from the primitive brain stem. It is completely automatic and we cannot prevent it. After a second or two, we can usually figure out the source of the noise and assess the danger. Then we can make an informed decision on what action to take.

This wonderful decision-making ability is a function of the larger sections of our brain and allows us to choose what we do about the automatic stimuli. It allows us to exercise "self control." The automatic reflex is the same one that any organism feels at the first glimpse of a charging predator or the sound of running footsteps behind them. The ability to make the subsequent choices is uniquely human.

The maternal instinct is another example of a necessary and beneficial instinct. Mothers of all species automatically love and protect their babies. It's the most natural thing in the world. They don't have to weigh the alternatives and make a decision. The few women who abandon or kill their babies are either emotionally or mentally deficient or, for some reason, are making a conscious decision to override the normal feeling of a mother's love for her child.

We still have several instincts that were once very beneficial and even necessary but serve no useful purpose in a civilized world. In fact, some are downright detrimental to the human species. Acting on instincts such as aggression, territoriality and dominance has had very destructive consequences such as war, slavery, torture, murder and racial and ethnic prejudice.

Scientists have said that we have "dangerous evolutionary baggage" and the violent history of our species should be ample evidence that we need to be aware of this baggage and do something about it. All adult humans, unless somehow mentally impaired, have the decision-making power to intelligently handle any of these tendencies. Some we control every day and others we obey without question because, at the time, it just feels like the right thing to do.

CHAPTER 4

War, Aggression, Territoriality

How can we recognize instinctive behavior in humans? Most individual human actions are made after thinking about alternatives and making decisions based on various inputs. Instinctive behavior is simply acting on a feeling with no thought about whether it is right or wrong or what effect it will have on us or anyone else. We often choose to ignore even strong feelings and urges, so it is very difficult to determine whether any particular action is instinctive or the result of a conscious decision. Also, some people make conscious decisions to follow an urge no matter how wrong it is or how much it will hurt someone.

However, if we study any number of other species that have little or no ability to make decisions, patterns that are common to all of them become readily apparent and we can recognize them as instinctive. Then we can compare these to large-scale human behavior patterns to see if there are any similarities. Studying any species provides insights but species that hunt and eat meat are the most informative because humans evolved from a long line of predators.

The studies must be done with the species in their native habitat in the true survival mode. Studies done on domesticated animals, or animals in captivity, are of limited value because these animals are no longer in their natural habitat and their behavior is modified accordingly.

One of the most easily observable, common traits of animals in the wild is that they live in groups. Group size varies between species but they are all relatively small, generally between 10 and 100. The groups may be referred to by a variety of names such as packs, clans, families, tribes, herds etc. Each group normally has an established territory where they forage and hunt for food. They fiercely defend this territory against invaders and often give their lives to protect it.

Surprisingly, the invaders are normally neighboring groups of the same species. An outside observer can't see any difference, but each group knows exactly who their friends and enemies are. All strangers are enemies so the group mentality is basically, "It's us against everybody else." Many species mark their territory with scent or some other indicator that clearly serves as a "No Trespassing" sign.

Since there is often not enough food for everyone, all groups seek to expand their territories. This expansion literally means driving off or killing all male members of a neighboring group. Normally, females and infants are allowed to live and may become part of the new group.

How and why did this strategy of living in relatively small, highly competitive groups become so prevalent and so important to the improvement and survival of so many species? None of the ancient organisms that developed this instinct had any choice in the matter. The inborn traits that provided an advantage endured because only the creatures that inherited them survived.

The intense competition between groups insured that only the strongest and smartest individuals got to live long enough to reproduce. The sick, lame, weak or otherwise disadvantaged were weeded out before they could pass on any inferior traits so the species gene pool constantly improved. In the cold, hard world of the "survival of the fittest," there is no mercy or compassion, no "right to life," only grim reality.

Early humans existed in this type of environment, but not for long. The advantages of walking upright and having a large brain and opposable thumbs soon led to tool and weapon making. Since that time, humans have not been in the "survival of the fittest" mode. The sick, lame and disadvantaged are cared for and kept alive. The strongest, healthiest, and smartest humans in the world can be easily killed by a weak, sick or mentally impaired person with a weapon. Essentially all humans reproduce and pass on both good and bad genes.

Years ago, before anthropologists had done long-term studies of creatures in the wild, it was assumed that animals within a species did not actually kill one another except perhaps by accident. It was known that all animals fought a lot but it seemed that the losers normally just ran off and escaped with their lives. We now have proof that this old assumption is not true.

While it is true that members within an established group of animals rarely kill one another, all species will kill members of rival groups if they can. Normally, that is very difficult because individuals, especially adult males, are so equally matched and have the same claws, fangs, teeth and strength for weapons. Usually it comes down to superior numbers and the larger group wins. Chimpanzees have been observed and even filmed systematically murdering all male members and sometimes females and young of a neighboring group to expand their territory.

For centuries it was assumed that one of the major differences between humans and animals was that we killed our own kind but animals did not. Some older people may remember hearing or reading that when they were young. Before we had weapons, our ancestors often tried to kill other humans with their bare hands but, of course, the casualty rate was much lower. It is obvious now that we humans are simply exhibiting aggressive behavior that is common to all species but we are much more successful and efficient killers now that we have invented weapons.

The history of life on earth in the "survival of the fittest" environment is an epic struggle against tremendous odds. All species had to be relatively prolific to insure that a few would survive and carry on. Because of numerous adversities such as disease, predation, accidents, drought etc, the birth rate had to be very high. In favorable conditions all species have the reproductive capability to quickly overpopulate their home territory.

Most species that have ever existed are now extinct and some, such as dinosaurs, are excellent examples of species that had a long successful run but are no longer around.

The first dinosaurs were fairly small but at the time they first appeared they were the largest and most efficient predators on land. With no natural enemies they automatically went to the top of the food chain and their only competition was there own kind. In this type of competition, many find it much easier to move to areas that other members of their species have not yet discovered rather than try to take over territory that is already inhabited.

Moving to open territory was quite easy because, at that time, the continents were all jammed together into one huge landmass that we refer to as Pangea (all earth). It was centered in the topical latitudes so the entire area was warm enough for the cold-blooded reptiles. In a short time, perhaps only a few centuries, the early dinosaurs inhabited all the land in the world. That is why we find dinosaur fossils on every continent today.

Once the dinosaurs ran out of expansion room, the competition for existing resources really got serious. It was literally eat or be eaten. Any chance mutation that provided some type of advantage, however small, became the difference between survival and reproduction and early death. The arms race was on. Small differences in climate and topography favored different mutations and led to many different dinosaur species, both plant eaters and meat eaters.

As Pangea started to break up into separate continents, land and sea barriers caused more isolation and climate changes created more varied habitats. As creatures adapted to these new habitats they evolved into new species, capable of thriving in their respective environments. Early mammals also existed during this time but they were small, nocturnal creatures forced to hide underground during the day when the fierce reptiles roamed in search of food.

One or more gigantic asteroids that struck the earth about 65 million years ago caused massive destruction and a decrease in global temperature that contributed to the extinction of at least one-fourth of all existing species in the sea as well as on land. None of the large reptiles survived so a wide variety of habitats suddenly became available to the tiny, warm-blooded mammals that needed very little food and were able to tolerate the colder temperatures. They proliferated, populated the vast, unoccupied areas and began adapting to a host of new environments. The long, successful reign of the dinosaurs had ended and the age of mammals had begun.

The story of our species has some striking similarities to the dinosaur saga. As soon as we invented tools and weapons, we became the predator at the top of the food chain with no serious natural enemies except our own kind. Mastering fire was another significant advantage which allowed us to live in any climate.

Our initial migration out of Africa started around eighty thousand years ago and in time we populated the entire planet. It was not a peaceful, orderly migration nor was it bloodless. After the first travelers settled a new land, all subsequent groups had to either drive them out or bypass them until all habitable areas were occupied. After that, the competition got even more serious.

Groups that adapted to their new territory and successfully defended it for a few generations considered it their sacred land, given to them by some mystical power or force of nature. Most groups had a name for their own members that essentially means "the people" and a name for all other people that translates roughly to mean "the barbarians," indicative of the age-old "it's us against everyone else" mentality.

With no written history, myth and legend often based on dreams explained how they became the original and rightful owners of their land. In truth, at any particular moment in time, the inhabitants of any area are simply the latest group that has succeeded in driving out, absorbing or otherwise eliminating the previous inhabitants. It is what all species instinctively do.

As a species we have a long history of conquering neighboring countries and expanding empires. We tend to laud and revere the winners, both those who survived and those who didn't, but generally we're not really concerned about the losers. Until recently, we just didn't know better. Now science has proven that the origin of all this invading and conquering comes from some old outdated instincts and has shown us some much better alternatives. It should be so simple to choose the peaceful, intelligent alternatives.

With the advent of civilization and the proliferation of humans, the practice of living in groups and fighting to the death with neighboring groups is no longer necessary for our survival. In fact, it's just the opposite because it causes so much death and destruction. And yet, there are millions of people still doing it.

There are examples all over the world, but perhaps some of the most obvious are in third world countries. For instance, why are some African tribes such as the Tutsis and the Hutus at war? Why do they kill and commit horrible atrocities on neighbors? To an outsider, both tribes are exactly alike, *but everyone in each group knows who the enemy is.*

Why were so many Kurds in Iraq slaughtered by fellow Iraqis? They wanted to become a separate nation with their own little territory where they could have their own culture and practice their own interpretation of the Moslem faith. Why do the Palestinians want a separate state? They could just become citizens of Syria or Jordan or even Israel and have quiet, peaceful lives.

Why did all the satellite countries surrounding Russia assert their independence when the Communist government collapsed? Surely, staying with a new and improved Russia and forming a kind of United States of Asia would have been more beneficial to everyone. Think of what Africa could be if everyone there quit fighting and worked together as one nation. But that would be going against human nature. That would mean overriding our basic instincts.

In the United States, why did the South secede from the North and establish a separate nation? They knew it would lead to civil war. That didn't matter at all. In fact, to many, it was a reason to celebrate. At last, they had their own nation where they could have their own culture, including slavery, without interference. They were eager for the chance to kill the "damn Yankees" to establish that separatism and they were more than willing to sacrifice their own lives to defend it

Why did the French-speaking people of eastern Canada try to become a separate country? They were just trying to become a smaller, more manageable, more homogenous group with their own customs and, of course, French as the national language. Had they succeeded, they too would certainly have been ready to kill former neighbors to defend their territory.

Where does the "lynch-mob mentality" come from? When the "fury of the mob" is aroused, is there any rational thought going on or is it simply the unrestrained response to our instinct of aggression against an enemy? The enemy has been captured and deserves to die. Murdering captives has been a common practice throughout the history of our species. A few of the mob members may have second thoughts afterward but at the time, it felt like the right thing to do.

The list of questions is literally endless. Why did some European countries build empires by conquering and colonizing other countries? The answer is simply "because they could." When the Europeans came to the New World, it was entirely populated by a single race of people who lived in separate tribes and made war on each other. There was no national unity or cooperation on the scale necessary to repel the invaders. A small number of great chiefs such as Pontiac and Tecumseh were able to unite some of the tribes for a while but after a few years the confederations fell apart and the rivalry continued even as the Europeans were taking over the country.

On all levels, people have always been warring with other people. From families and clans such as the Hatfields and the McCoys to the World Wars, it's what we do. It's what we've always done! In fact, it's what all species have always done. We have used a variety of minor human differences such as color, race, religion, culture, and language to define the enemy, and once defined, the enemy must be killed or conquered.

History shows that, with time, enemies can become friends and allies. What changed? What makes a hated, reviled enemy who deserved to die turn into a friend? And what turns a friend into an enemy? Why are there always plenty of enemies to go around? Why is it so easy to find things to hate in people?

Why is warfare such an integral part of our lives? Why is war glorified and revered? Many different people have come up with strikingly similar answers to these questions, all very earnest and patriotic. The vast majority emphasize "we must defend our country" or "we must protect our way of life."

The real answer, of course, is simply, "it's our nature." It just feels right at the time. But why don't we collectively stop it? After all, we are humans and we can choose not to participate. We can "just say no" to violence. Individuals have been overriding instincts for centuries. Individuals and groups have always protested against war. Unfortunately, there are never enough protesters and the majority rules. There seems to be no decline in warfare on any scale.

War is such an accepted part of all societies that almost all countries have standing armies and many people even make careers out of being soldiers. The rationale for having a military force is always for "defense purposes only" but if that were literally true for all countries, there would be no invasions to defend against and therefore no wars. The definition of "defending our country" is often expanded to include pre-emptive strikes and reclaiming areas that once may have been part of a certain realm or territory, but were somehow lost.

The fact that some countries have little or no military force and maintain a policy of strict neutrality is evidence that many people wish for a world without war. The establishment of the United Nations is another sure sign. The original concept of the UN was that differences could be negotiated and invasions prevented through dialogue and compromise or if that failed, a show of unity against the potential aggressor. It has not been very successful, primarily because of "human nature."

The reality of the UN is that there is little unity and only limited cooperation. Some nations are ruled by ruthless, self-serving dictators and many are trying to cope with internal strife and warring factions that want to split an already small country into several smaller countries. Relatively few member nations have any real history of freedom and civil rights and many of the leaders have only disdain for the concept of democracy.

In the face of all this, it would be foolhardy for most countries to do away with their military forces unless all countries agreed to do the same and then honored the agreement. Given what we know about human nature, is that reasonable? Not at the present time, but something has to change or eventually some fanatic will resort to widespread biological warfare or nuclear weapons.

One old argument in favor of warfare says, "Yes, wars are costly in terms of lives and property but look at all the technology they produce that we wouldn't otherwise have." This seems to be a misguided rationalization since a large percentage of the advances gained this way have led to more and better weapons of destruction. Compare that to the stunning technological advances of the 1960s and 70s that came from the concentrated effort to send manned spacecraft to the moon and unmanned craft to the rest of our Solar System.

Surely, putting a third or even a fourth of the resources expended for making war into constructive pursuits such as space exploration, alternate energy sources and planetary ecology would generate more and better technology than armed conflict. If only we could get past our tendency to make war.

All of the major religions of the world teach peace and tolerance. They have certainly made progress toward influencing people to be nicer to one another. Sadly however, religion is not enough. Too many wars have been fought in the name of religion and countless atrocities have been committed by religious people on millions of other people because of their religious beliefs.

The vast majority of men and women who have fought in wars were devoutly religious. Almost without exception, suicide bombers are fanatically religious and many terrorists claim to be part of a holy mission against enemies of their God.

So what is the answer? Is there any way to convince the majority of the world population to stop this pointless carnage and just live and let live? Maybe not, but surely to make any progress at all, everyone should know why we have this warlike, combative aspect of our nature.

If enough people understand and realize that dominance and aggression are just ancient, primal instincts that were once necessary but have long since outlived their usefulness, maybe we would all simply choose not to fight. Do we really need more dead and disabled people, grieving families, murdered, maimed and orphaned children, destruction, pain and grief? Don't we have enough of that from natural causes?

Do we really need more of this?

31

And this?

"Up to now, aggression has been an attribute with definite survival advantages. Now, however, it may destroy us if we cannot control our instincts with our reason."

Stephen Hawking

CHAPTER 5

Dominance and Submission

Dominance and submission may appear to be two separate traits but they are actually two parts of the same instinct, like the two sides of a coin. Behavior patterns reflecting this double-sided instinct are quite easy to see and interpret.

Actions that demonstrate dominance include staring, swaggering, flexing, snarling, bristling, threatening, puffing up to appear larger, charging and flailing of limbs. Submission is indicated by averting the eyes, lowering the head, silence or whining, crouching, bowing, kneeling, groveling and exposing ones throat and underbelly.

Within any homogenous group, regardless of species, there is an established dominance hierarchy normally headed by an alpha male. Under the alpha, the other adult males achieve their status as beta, gamma, delta etc. according to size, strength and confidence. Normally, the females and the youngsters are at the bottom.

In some species, one or more females may attain relatively high positions but, because of sheer size and brute strength, the alpha is normally always a male. There are a few notable exceptions such as hyenas in which the female is stronger and, in those cases, the alphas are female. All individuals in the group know and accept their place. This "pecking order" system is very efficient for maintaining peace and harmony. All members know who they must submit to and who they can dominate without fear of reprisal.

Of course, the hierarchy doesn't stay the same for long. Most members, especially adult males, are striving to advance their rank and, if they keep moving up, eventually they challenge the alpha. Even the mightiest of alphas can't stay at the top as they age and lose their strength.

The fights that occur within a group to establish the ranking are quite different from the life and death battles with neighboring groups. They consist mostly of noise and threats with very little actual violence and only rarely result in serious injury or death. The loser is usually convinced in a very short time to either retreat or demonstrate submission in some other manner. The winner is satisfied and stops the attack. There appears to be no rancor or hard feelings.

Losers, even deposed alphas, usually accept the lower rank and stay within the group. Loners in a predatory environment do not survive long. Individual positions in a group may change frequently but the entire group is always keenly aware of the current rankings.

The benefits of being an alpha are readily apparent. He gets first choice of available food and water supplies, the best meat from a fresh kill and the respect and adoration of the rest of the group. He also gets to mate with all the fertile females, which insures that only the best genes are passed on to the offspring.

Of course, the alpha has some heavy responsibilities also. His mere presence must calm and comfort the group and inspire feelings of confidence, security and loyalty. He must be skilled in tracking and killing prey to feed the group. Hunting is a cooperative effort of adult males of all ranks and some ability is innate, but the group members must also learn techniques from their leader.

The alpha is the first line of defense against invaders and predators and must be in the forefront of all battles. This too, is a cooperative effort. All adult males fight in all battles and often sacrifice their lives in the process. The alpha must also know when the group needs to expand its territory and must lead the charge to invade a new area and conquer a neighboring group.

The hierarchy is not limited to the adult males. Adult females have an established order also. In fact, the term "pecking order" originated from studies of hens. In general, females are subordinate to males but mothers often dominate their sons well into adulthood. Some things never change! The young also have their own rankings, usually determined by age and gender.

Dominance and submission in humans is also relatively easy to recognize. Individual behavior isn't always as clear-cut as in other species but large-scale group behavior is quite clear. Military organizations are excellent examples of highly structured, governmental departments that utilize and rely on these traits. All group members know their job and their rank and most are striving for promotions. They all show the appropriate deference to anyone of higher rank and dominate anyone of lower rank. Command and control are the utmost priority and there is little serious dissension at any level.

The majority of humans, especially in wartime, are willing and even eager to do their share of the fighting. These attributes along with bravery and self-sacrifice are the keys to military success. The technology and the weapons may be new but the organizational framework and the individual mindset is ancient.

Perhaps even better examples can be seen in gangs. Organized crime generally consists of groups and families with well-defined territories. There is an alpha male at the top of each group with several levels of soldiers below him and women and children below the soldiers. All members, including the soldiers, show obvious signs of submission to the alpha and others of higher rank, but they all cooperate to defend their territory or invade a rival gangs territory. In fact, many give their lives in this way. Often, one or more of the soldiers challenge the alpha. Because of modern weapons, these contests are no longer decided by physical strength and normally result in several deaths.

There are countless other examples of gang structure that clearly exhibit the dominance hierarchy. This behavior is so common that it cannot be the result of well thought out decisions by millions of individuals. It must be instinctive behavior that is being acted out rather than overridden by rational thought and conscious effort.

There are many examples of these traits in everyday life that are generally not as violent as gang behavior. For centuries, fathers and stepfathers have assumed the role of the alpha male in family units. The saying "A mans home is his castle" implies that men are absolute rulers in their homes and many have acted accordingly.

Parents must dominate their children to a certain degree to keep them safe until they are ready to go out on their own but, clearly, even this necessary manifestation of dominance must be tempered with reason and logic to prevent going overboard.

Far too many people, primarily men, seem to lack the ability to determine a proper response to childish behavior. Physical abuse has led to numerous incidents of serious injury and even death to helpless children. Psychological abuse and neglect have caused many others both short term and long term emotional problems in their progression into adulthood. Role models have a significant effect on developing personalities and children of abusive parents often lack the necessary restraint to keep from being abusive adults.

Throughout human history, males have always instinctively felt that they should be able to dominate females. In modern times, many men suppress these feelings, at least part of the time and most women strive for equality or even dominance, at least part of the time. Still, there are unmistakable signs. Males far outnumber females in positions of power and leadership in government and business.

Corporate structure all over the world reflects almost total male dominance. Governments of developed countries have made notable progress in equality by establishing equal opportunity and fair hiring practices but there is much resistance. As a rule, humans do not willingly give up positions of real or implied power.

Men who stop participating in certain masculine activities because of wives or girlfriends may be referred to as "henpecked" by both men and women. When a male and female are traveling together in any moving conveyance from a horse and buggy to an airplane, the male is almost always at the controls. This is true even if the female owns the vehicle. It just seems more natural that way.

In democratic societies, one of the notable milestones in women's fight for equality is the privilege of voting in national elections. It takes more than voting rights to ensure equality but it is a positive and necessary step. The chronology of this milestone is actually more recent than most of us realize.

The island nation of New Zealand was the only country to grant universal suffrage to women prior to 1900. In the United States, voting rights were legally extended to black males after the Civil War but women were not included until 1920. It may come as a surprise to many of the current citizens of the US that there are still quite a few people living here who were born before all women were granted this basic democratic right.

Male domination has been a fact of life for women since the beginning of our species and will not change quickly. The positive changes that we see occurring in free societies do not extend to most dictatorships, monarchies and theocracies.

Movies can be compared to mini time capsules that reflect the overall trends and mindsets of the mainstream of society at the time they were filmed. It has only been in the last decade of the twentieth century that significant numbers of women have been portrayed in movies as strong, independent thinkers fully as capable as men. Prior to that, female roles were primarily as vamps, gold diggers, trophies, sex objects or simply bits of fluff in need of male guidance and protection.

All the old movies that are now available on cable or satellite TV plainly depict the subordinate female status. Newer movies in the more progressive societies show women in a variety of nontraditional roles indicating they are gaining more and more acceptance as equals.

Also, significant changes in modern marriage vows are clear indicators of this changing attitude. For centuries traditional marriage vows in most churches have contained verbiage that requires brides to "submit to," "be subordinate to" or "obey" their husbands. Today these terms are rarely used in wedding ceremonies.

Christianity's Tenth Commandment requires that men do not covet their neighbor's possessions, which is a wonderful rule. But, clearly here, the neighbor is a man and some of the "possessions" listed specifically in the Commandment include his wife, his slaves or servants, and his animals. Was this literally the original wording on the tablets or has something been altered in one of the many translations of Biblical history? Realistically, wives are not possessions and slavery is not condoned by any religion.

In a true "survival of the fittest" environment, physical strength is the primary determinant in a dominance hierarchy, which automatically puts all females below all adult males. With the advent of civilization, other factors such as intelligence, education, talent, skill, drive and aptitude have become primary. In theory, this provides equal opportunity to both sexes but in practice, male dominated societies find it very painful to share positions of power and influence with women regardless of their ability.

True equality for women is slowly becoming a reality in the more progressive societies of developed countries. Sadly, for millions of women in less progressive countries it is only a dream, a myth that they hear about occasionally but never experience.

Probably since at least the beginning of civilization, duties have been divided into the traditional "man's work and woman's work." With modern tools and weapons, most women are fully capable of mastering almost any previously all-male job if they have the inclination and the opportunity. This became abundantly clear during the Second World War when women from essentially all of the involved countries stepped up and produced the machines and armaments needed by both sides.

During the German campaign into Russia, a group of Soviet women formed a makeshift bomber squadron using the only available planes, a few obsolete bi-wing primary trainers that could carry two small bombs each. Night after night they flew multiple missions over the German lines dropping their bombs on equipment, supplies and troop encampments. They developed brilliant tactics in their low and slow aircraft to evade ground fire and to outmaneuver the fighters that came to intercept them.

Many of these brave women flew over a thousand missions with almost no loss of pilots and aircraft. They were so successful that the Germans gave them the name "Nachthexen" (Night Witches) and viewed them with a mixture of fear and respect. Stalin was so impressed that he formed three squadrons of female fighter pilots who flew first line fighter aircraft also on night missions.

In the United States, women participated in all aspects of the war except combat. Women in military auxiliary units flew the test flights on the fighters and bombers as they rolled off the assembly lines and then ferried them to bases both stateside and overseas. Only recently have those women received the long overdue recognition they deserved.

After the war, women were expected to go back to their dependent roles as wives and mothers but many refused and continued a growing push for equality and opportunity. Progressive countries have done the most to further their cause. In the last half of the twentieth century, more and more women have been successful in operating businesses and moving into previously "all male" jobs such as police officers, firefighters, long haul truckers, astronauts, etc. Most have had to battle some degree of sexism from male co-workers who saw them as a threat.

In some societies, male dominance is absolute. Any male is allowed and even expected to punish, maim or kill a female family member who has said or done something considered to be wrong. Even women who have been raped may be driven out or killed because in some way it is perceived to be their fault. The males normally feel quite justified in these actions and rarely have feelings of pity or compassion, only anger and revenge. After all, she disobeyed!

All humans have this two-sided instinct but the two sides are not always equal. Many people lean more toward one side than the other. If the dominant side is stronger, the person will most likely act on those feelings and suppress the urge to be submissive.

Conversely, one who tends to be submissive is more likely to suppress the urge to dominate. We can all think of several people who fall into each category. A more dominant person wants to be in charge and may be described as a doer, a leader, a hard-nose or a bully. A more submissive person may be referred to as needy, dependent, clingy, timid or a follower.

People like Ivan the Terrible, Hitler, Saddam Hussein and Idi Amin are extreme examples of what humans are capable of when they have absolute power and feel there will be no retribution. Serial killers, such as Ted Bundy, John Wayne Gacy and "Son of Sam" fit into this category, also. Murder, torture and enslavement are ultimate expressions of dominance and control.

Cults often contain both types of people. Leaders such as Jim Jones and David Koresh are classic examples of men driven to become the alpha male. Their submissive followers felt a strong need for a leader who would literally take responsibility for their lives, make all their decisions and show them the way. They did exactly what they were told and when the end was near, they either committed suicide or made no effort to save themselves or their children. There are many suitable places for needy, submissive people in any society but if they are attracted to a radical cult, a hate group or some other fringe organization they may pay a heavy price.

The hate groups that form in any free society are all remarkably similar, no matter whom they define as the enemy. They may target people of a certain race, creed, color, religion, culture, ethnic background or sexual orientation. Many groups define more than one of these characteristics as evil, loathsome and entirely unacceptable to the "normal," "righteous" or "superior" people.

The leaders of these groups all have several traits in common, the primary one being a driving need to be a leader, to be in charge. They are usually charismatic and persuasive and appear to be very intelligent, knowledgeable and sincere. The rhetoric sounds very reasonable and authentic to people who are easily swayed or who were already inclined to believe in a certain way. The leaders know how to inflame and exploit the primitive instinct of aggression against the vile enemy.

Rage and hate seem to be integral parts of our primitive instincts of war, aggression and dominance. Acting together, they can literally override all traces of fear, caution and self-preservation. They are an important part of the "killer instinct" that enables us to be fierce and fearless warriors and to kill other humans in battle without remorse or compassion. In most species, with the unfortunate exception of humans, these primitive emotions normally surface only in the heat of battle.

Killing has always been a part of life for all species but stalking and killing prey for food involves a totally different set of instincts. A cat that captures a mouse displays no hint of anger or malice. If it is not very hungry it may even toy with the doomed animal. It is simply playing with its quarry and exhibits no emotion except perhaps amusement.

But let another cat try to take the mouse and instantly everything changes. Adrenalin flows, weapons are bared, caution is forgotten, battle cries are sounded and the feline version of hate and rage become evident. The mouse may even escape but that is no longer important. Various versions of confrontations like this occur constantly in all species.

Humans can choose to keep these destructive emotions active in their minds as long as they wish and their personalities and lifestyles may clearly reflect their choice. We all know several people whom we could describe as "angry." If unchecked, this mindset can consume a person and lead to bitterness and physical as well as psychological debilitation. It can also result in violence, cruelty, misery and death. The object of our rage may be vile and loathsome but giving in to these emotions is literally empowering someone else to influence us and even to have some measure of control over us. This cannot be good.

There are plenty of "bad guys" in the world who deserve our hate, rage and other negative feelings. But for us to hate, look down on, or cause any harm whatsoever to the good people of the earth who happen to have some superficial difference such as race, religion, culture or sexual preference is a gross misapplication of our human values. At the very least it is a monumental waste of our time, talent and energy.

Sports seem to be a natural, healthy outlet for feelings of aggression, competition and dominance. Individual sports probably started within established groups of early humans as an extension of the normal struggle for rank and position in the dominance hierarchy.

Team sports soon followed when thinking people in neighboring groups realized that some rivalry issues could be settled by a few individuals doing battle with an enemy team. Initially, the losing team was probably killed but as the lives of family and friends became more precious, rules were developed to make the contests safer.

A practice called "counting coup" was used by some Native American tribes and is an excellent example of a bloodless way of establishing power and dominance. A warrior would charge an enemy group, and simply touch one or more of them with his weapon and get back to his own group with no loss of life. The message was clear; "I could have killed you but I didn't." Such bravery was admired and respected by friend and foe alike and probably settled disputes, prevented battles and saved lives.

Children of all ages exhibit signs of both dominance and submission. Normally, older children dominate younger ones but even in peer groups of the same age, there are leaders and followers. Some individuals become leaders by using intelligence and persuasion and others by bullying, but every group establishes some sort of a dominance hierarchy. Dominating behavior becomes more evident in the absence of adult supervision.

Some aspects of this instinct are obviously not only no longer useful, but are actually harmful. Still, there are also several positive aspects such as ambition, thirst for knowledge, striving for excellence and the drive to succeed. These are the wholesome, honorable ways we get promotions, the way we move up the ladder and improve our positions in the hierarchy of our society. The rewards are usually more money, nicer things, more leisure time, more control over our lives and generally a more satisfying life.

Negative aspects such as ruthless ambition, greed, lying, cheating and murder have also been used to achieve power and control. This ancient tendency can be very destructive unless channeled into peaceful activities. Our need for control should be used to control ourselves. The only person you can and should control is you. That is a very big job for most of us, but one worth doing. We can do it because we are special, we are human beings.

People with a strong need to dominate are not happy people, in fact, they are normally quite angry. The dominator may achieve temporary satisfaction from forcing someone to do something but it's never exactly right. The timing may be poor, the task may be incomplete, the attitude may be wrong. Something is still lacking.

You seldom, if ever, see an obviously dominant/submissive couple where either one is happy. Many of these relationships result in spousal abuse, divorce or even murder. Happy couples generally regard each other as equals and do not act on these natural feelings of need for power and control.

Most people feel the instinct of dominance every day but perhaps do not recognize it as such. We have all experienced situations when we say aloud or to ourselves, "If I were the boss, I would make some big changes." The particular circumstances are not important here. The important thing is that this feeling is common to all of us. It literally translates to, "*If I had the power* I would shape those people up and make them do right."

But what is "right?" Invariably, it is what "I" think is right because "I" see things the way they really are. We may not even practice what we preach, but we can easily see what is best for other people. "If I only had the power!" It's no coincidence that we all have these feelings. It's part of being human.

Road rage is another common reaction. Why do we get so angry when other drivers get in our way or do something unexpected that we don't like? Why do we feel like running them over? It's not something we decide to feel, it just happens instantly. We instinctively want the power to punish them and get them off the road and out of our way. We can't help the reaction but we can control what we do about it.

Another typical example is when men gather in a bar, pool hall or similar place, there is likely to be at least one fight. As long as it's a fair fight with no weapons, it usually ends peaceably. The loser acknowledges defeat in some obvious manner, normally before he is seriously hurt. The winner, having established his dominance, graciously accepts the submission. They may even shake hands and become friends. This is typical male behavior.

Modern weapons, especially guns, have made these dominance and control encounters much more dangerous. If either or both men are armed, even a small disagreement may result in serious injury or death, especially if alcohol is involved. A gun enables any human, regardless of size, strength or mental capacity, to establish the ultimate dominance over any other human.

The previous scenarios are quite common. They occur because of human responses to the old instincts of competition and dominance, but modern weapons have made such contests much more serious and more likely to be fatal.

The mere existence of guns, as well as other weapons of destruction, should be a giant red flag, a wake-up call to all humans that says, this dominance thing is something we need to get a handle on and keep under control. There are many safe outlets for this ancient calling. Almost any competition that does no harm to others, such as sports, debate, striving for excellence at work or other areas of interest will satisfy any normal person.

Rape and pedophilia are prime examples of uncontrolled dominant behavior. They certainly have nothing to do with love. The primary motivation is the feeling of absolute power and control over another human being, with a side benefit of sexual gratification. Children are targeted because they are completely helpless. They do not have the strength, knowledge or experience to protect themselves. Women generally do not have the strength to fend off an attacker either.

For the protection of the innocent, there should be no such thing as "known sex offenders" at large in society. Depending on the type and severity of their crimes, they should either be in a rehabilitation program with a superb success rate, incarcerated for life in a prison or an appropriate mental institution or executed.

Rehabilitation, so far, has been remarkably unsuccessful. With more effort and expense, this could be greatly improved, but as thinking, compassionate humans we must become more concerned about the rights of the innocent than with the rights of the predators.

For reasons which elude most parents, pedophilia seems to be viewed as a petty crime by many justice systems. If the victims aren't killed the perpetrators usually get off with fairly light sentences. It almost appears that in the eyes of the law, and for that matter, some church officials, the pedophile is simply choosing the wrong people for a little harmless sex. While it may possibly be that simple for a few of these disgusting perverts, the primary motive for far too many of them is not sex but physical and emotional dominance of another human.

A significant number of pedophiles eventually find that mere sexual domination is not enough and they move on to the ultimate domination;

murder often preceded by torture. Others may feel that they cannot let the victim live for fear of being exposed as a predator.

Regardless of their motives, pedophiles are responsible for the deaths of far too many children. Even one death is too many and then there is the severe emotional distress of countless others in relation to these crimes that must be considered. Pedophilia should be recognized as a crime that is every bit as serious as murder.

Concerned parents all over the United States are trying to get tougher laws passed to deal with these despicable predators but progress seems painfully slow. Highly publicized tragedies have led to some positive results such as "Megan's Law" which initiates several quick-response measures as soon as a child is reported missing. A national database of known child molesters is being established and some authorities have pledged more vigorous enforcement of the "known sex offender" registration requirement.

All this is encouraging but far too many known child molesters simply move to new areas and do not register with local law enforcement. Much more effort is needed to institutionalize these perverts or, at the very least, make sure that everyone in the entire country knows their names, what they have done, what they look like and where they live.

The long-running, weekly television show "America's Most Wanted" is an outstanding example of how criminals can be apprehended when they are showcased on national TV. The show's host, John Walsh, was instrumental in creating it after his own young son, Adam, was kidnapped and murdered in 1981.

Mr. Walsh spends much of his free time actively campaigning for tougher laws against pedophiles and more vigorous enforcement of existing laws such as the registration requirement. He also takes advantage of every opportunity for public speaking to inform parents and children of the tactics used by predators and sponsors programs at all levels to educate people on how they can avoid becoming victims. His tireless efforts have undoubtedly saved many lives and prevented much sorrow and emotional anguish. Sadly, many children are still being molested and murdered.

Other proactive movie and TV personalities have used their celebrity status to focus the attention of lawmakers on these heinous crimes against innocent children. One of the most notable is Oprah Winfrey who was instrumental in getting the law passed that requires child molesters to register with authorities wherever they go.

After a few years it became evident that this law was not stringent enough and since then she has dedicated entire episodes of her popular afternoon talk show to showcase pedophiles and expose them to millions of viewers. The majority of her viewers are women with children or grandchildren, who may or may not watch shows such as "Americas Most Wanted."

Ms Winfrey has also personally pledged $100,000 to anyone providing information that leads to the capture of a pedophile. Viewer tips have led to the arrest of several accused perverts within a few days of their exposure on her show. This is another shining example of a dedicated individual using star power for a very worthy cause.

The Internet has proven to be a real boon for pedophiles. Teens and pre-teens eagerly share their private lives and thoughts with unseen strangers on the net. Many of the contacts young people make are men who are trolling the net for victims. For a variety of reasons, a significant percentage of parents are unaware of the risks their children are taking. Even when parents are aware, few know what to do about it other than warn and threaten their children and hope for the best.

NBC's Dateline has conducted several sting operations to showcase and expose on-line predators. A group of highly motivated adults, known as "Perverted Justice," pretended to be children chatting on the web sites targeted by the predators. They invited the men who wrote sexually explicit dialogue to come to a house in the suburbs to meet the "child" they had been communicating with. The house was equipped with hidden TV cameras.

Once inside the men were confronted by NBC reporter, Chris Hansen, who questioned them at length about their intentions and their sexually explicit on-line language. Most had even sent photos of their genitalia to the people they thought were children. Some ran away but most stayed and tried to lie about their motives for being there.

The first two operations were conducted without law enforcement present but copies of the tapes were turned over to the authorities and, hopefully, were used to prosecute the offenders. The third sting was coordinated with the Police department of Riverside, California and fifty men were arrested in just three days.

The predators were all adult males ranging in age from nineteen to sixty-nine. Some were single and some were married. They represented all walks of life including schoolteachers, the clergy, law enforcement and, of course, known sex offenders.

This horrendous behavior cannot be attributed to natural human variations such as higher than normal sex drives. Many of the older men had brought some type of sexual performance enhancer such as Viagra. These perverts were seeking that elusive feeling of power and control over another human being and children were targeted because they are naïve, defenseless and easily dominated. Sexual release is simply a secondary benefit.

The most shocking aspect of this whole scenario is the sheer numbers of men who want to take advantage of children. The Riverside police department was literally overwhelmed. They had to call in off-duty personnel to handle the volume and most of the arrestees were from the local area. There is nothing to indicate that Riverside is all that different from any other small city. This suggests that there are staggering numbers of these perverts here in the United States and literally millions worldwide.

The sad fact is that the vast majority of these men are not mentally impaired. They could simply choose not to act on their vile fantasies. Instead, they choose to briefly live out these fantasies while inflicting untold physical and emotional scars on the unfortunate children and in some cases, the unsuspecting victims are even abducted and murdered.

Sadly, the fastest growing business on the Internet today is child pornography. Pedophiles are the ultimate buyers and apparently there are so many that the demand is enormous. Greedy, unprincipled people from all walks of life are cashing in by exploiting any accessible child. Incredibly, there are even some parents who are sacrificing their own children in a depraved quest for money.

Andrew Vachss, a well-known New York attorney, has dedicated his entire professional career to representing abused children. As such he is one of the foremost authorities on the inadequate ability of our legal system to deal effectively with both pedophiles and child pornographers.

Mr. Vachss is also an accomplished writer and one of his articles was featured in the February 19, 2006 issue of the Parade magazine, a Sunday supplement of most major newspapers. His insightful article describes the shocking scope of this deplorable business. He concludes the article with five crucial steps that must be taken to combat the growing menace to the children of the world. They include:

1. Significantly higher penalties for production and possession of child porn.
2. Abolishment of both the civil and criminal Statute of Limitations for pedophilia and child porn.
3. Enactment of Federal laws to enable the United States government to sue on behalf of any child depicted in pornographic material.
4. Recognition of child porn as an international civil rights crime and the use of all possible economic sanctions against countries that permit it.

5. Finally, he says that we must all take part in a massive effort to convince local, state and federal governments to commit the necessary funding and personnel to protect our country's most valuable resource, our children.

Bullying and senseless cruelty to animals also give the perpetrator a sense of power and control. Basically, those who hurt, maim or kill defenseless people or animals for their personal gratification are acting out uncontrolled responses to this ancient instinct of domination. The good news is that millions of people override this instinct every day. The bad news is that millions of us do not.

The big question here is, "Why do so many of us choose to override these instincts while others do not?" What is it that separates the good guys from the bad guys? Numerous factors are involved, including culture, upbringing, fear of reprisal, conscience, mental impairment, drugs or alcohol, and many others. Some of these factors will change with time but if everyone knew the source of these instinctive feelings, the majority of normal people would choose to ignore them.

Everyone would benefit if they realized that we have the same primitive brain stem as other species because it means that we really do have "animal instincts" which are a significant part of "human nature." These ancient instincts originated hundreds of millions of years ago and were retained and passed on to all subsequent species, including humans, because they were the ones that worked in the "survival of the fittest" environment.

Humans are no longer in that environment. Because of our large brains, we have been able to create civilization and because of our large brains, we can be civilized. We can be tolerant and understanding. All we have to do is consciously override or ignore some of our destructive "animal instincts" to improve our environment, our culture, our lives and the lives of others.

Capitalism in democracies around the world has led to rapid and wondrous advancements in most areas of human endeavor. It has provided almost unlimited opportunity for a large middle class of educated, productive, successful people. Unfortunately, all this opportunity has also resulted in some significant problems including pollution, poisoning of the environment and unconscionable waste of our natural resources. Clearly, the need for some restraint is required in capitalistic societies.

The inherent human instinct to dominate and succeed coupled with the drive to take care of "me and mine" first at the expense of all others has led to some gross inequities, excess wealth for some and grinding poverty for others.

Systems of government such as Socialism and Communism have been tried with the lofty sounding goals of security and equality for all citizens. As yet, no system has been completely successful because of "human nature." Any large scale softening of our combative, competitive natures will have to start with widespread knowledge of instinctive behavior combined with personal logic, reason and individual choice rather than by government decree.

Testosterone is one of the androgens shared by most species, at least all mammals, birds and reptiles. It is primarily a male hormone produced in the testes but females do produce small amounts. Many people think of it as merely a sex hormone and it is true that there is a direct correlation between testosterone level and sex drive, but its overall effect is much greater than that. It is also directly related to size, muscle mass, strength, stamina, aggression and fearlessness.

For hundreds of millions of years, males have needed these qualities to compete for alpha status and breeding rights. Those with higher levels were much more likely to leave descendants so all subsequent species, including humans, have inherited the tendency to produce a lot of this efficient performance enhancer. For men, peak production occurs in late teens and early twenties and slowly decreases with age. Steroids similar to testosterone are used by body builders and athletes to increase body mass, strength and stamina.

Testosterone has definitely been a mixed blessing for humans since the invention of weapons and the beginnings of civilization. Enhancement of the destructive alpha male traits of aggression and dominance has been a contributing factor in our history of violence, murder, slavery, destruction and rape. Higher levels of this hormone exaggerate all urges and emotions and make it more difficult for an individual to overcome and suppress the natural instinctive drive to conquer and dominate other humans.

We all have the ability to overcome any urge we may feel regardless of how much it is enhanced by testosterone but some men just have to be more determined than others. It is most difficult for teenage males because their hormone production is at it's peak and they have limited experience in suppressing and/or redirecting strong drives.

Young men are often restless, reckless, overly aggressive and rebellious with a strong drive to conquer and dominate. If they don't learn to deal with these enhanced tendencies, they are much more likely to become bullies, gang members, rapists and abusers of women.

In all other species, males with low levels of testosterone leave no offspring even if they survive until they are old enough to mate. Since there are so many humans and since essentially all of us get to mate and reproduce, testosterone levels vary much more in men than in males of any other species.

Many older men and even some younger men do not produce enough and must take supplemental doses by injection or the patch method to maintain a normal energy level and enjoy a satisfactory sex life. Supplements, such as Depo-testosterone and Delatestryl, are available in most developed countries for these men. These supplements were originally isolated from animal testes, primarily bulls, and are excellent examples of the many natural substances produced by other species that we can utilize because of our kinship with them.

Our kinship with other species has benefited us in many other ways as well. Doctors and scientists involved in medical research have used a variety of animals in laboratory tests that are considered too dangerous to be done on humans. The physiology of many mammals is close enough to ours to provide invaluable results before a product or treatment is approved for human use. Chimpanzees are widely used because their bodies are so similar to human bodies. In fact, 99.6% of our genes are exactly the same as chimp genes.

Rh factor was first recognized in the blood of *Rh*esus monkeys and later was found to also apply to other species including humans. Stem cell research is being conducted on several animal species. Organs and tissue from animals have been used in humans with some success and researchers are confident that they are close to solving the problems of growing suitable human organs in animals.

CHAPTER 6

Sex and Reproduction

In a true "Survival of the Fittest" environment, survival is only half the battle. The other half, reproduction, is what keeps the species going. For most of the last billion years the actions necessary for two organisms to combine their DNA to produce a new and separate organism has been controlled strictly by instinct. This is still true for most species. The relatively recent evolution of larger brains has allowed some species to make choices. Human sexual selection is primarily the result of conscious decision-making but there are clues to indicate that we are still influenced by instincts left over from ancient times.

The sex drive and the physiological changes that take place to allow mating, conception and birth are controlled by the primitive brain stem and require no decision-making. When a female reaches a certain age automatic hormonal changes are triggered in her body that set in motion specific cycles, enabling her to fulfill this crucial role in the survival of her species. At least one egg cell must be produced and physically moved to the area of her body where it can be fertilized by a male sperm cell.

When the egg is ready there must be some kind of signal to notify a specific male that the time is right for mating. The window of opportunity may be very short and timing is crucial. It is even more important to mate with the right male. In most species, females instinctively choose the alpha male and reject all others. This instinct insures that her offspring receive the best of the available male genes.

Scent was probably the one of the first signals used to signal female readiness and is still the primary indicator for most species today. When the time is optimal for conception females produce a specific scent that is an unmistakable signal to males. Human females have these same cycles and at times produce extra pheromones that can be detected, but scent has probably never been a primary indicator for humans. Long ago our ancestors began using visual cues to indicate sexual readiness.

When males of a species reach a certain age hormonal changes cause the production of sperm cells and awaken the ability to recognize female readiness signals. Males have always had to be ready to respond to female signals. Of course, in a "survival of the fittest" environment, many males never get to mate. They have to do a lot of fighting and winning to prove that they are worthy to pass on their genes. They must be the best of the best or the females will simply reject them. In species where groups are quite large, the females will also mate with high-ranking males other than the alpha.

Humans are subject to the same physical and physiological effects from automatically triggered hormones as other species. We also have the same instinctive responses to certain stimuli but human females are not limited to having sex only during certain times of their reproductive cycles. Long before humans evolved, our pre-human ancestors began having sex at any time, even when conception was not possible. This is not uniquely human as all primates do it.

Knowing about these instincts provides us with some clear insights into large-scale human sexual behavior. For instance, men are constantly looking at women. It is simply an automatic part of being male. The instinct was developed millions of years ago before any species had any decision-making ability. Males had to look at all females to determine if any were ready for mating so looking became the primary part of this instinct.

Males of all subsequent species, including humans, inherited this automatic response but just looking, in itself, was not arousing. Males constantly looked at all parts of the females bodies, including genitalia, and had no response if there were no female signals of readiness. But if the males saw a sign of sexual readiness, a secondary part of the instinct took over, hormones were released and the male was ready to mate.

For our pre-human ancestors, two visual cues became the primary indicators that triggered male response. One consisted of female movements and stance. Back then all species walked on all fours so arching the back downward and thrusting the buttocks upward, especially toward the male, became a sure signal. Human males still find this pose quite appealing and variations of it are used to advertise many products. We are all aware that "sex sells" almost anything and it's true. For instance, this advertisement is selling shoes.

Now, other than the obvious beauty of the model, what is so sexy about this picture? Since the vast majority of humans prefer front-to-front sex, logically this pose should have no particular appeal and yet, both men and women instinctively associate it with sexual readiness.

The other positive visual cue was a noticeable change in the appearance of the female genitalia. Back then, there was no such thing as foreplay so the female had to be fully aroused and ready to mate when a signal was displayed. At full arousal, the genital area became engorged with blood and the labia became red and swollen. This is common to all primates, including humans, but fossil evidence shows that by around three million years ago the first hominids started to walk upright.

This new stance effectively hid the genital area from view but these pre-human hominids had brains almost half as large as modern humans.

The new brain segments gave them the beginnings of the ability to think as well as some rudimentary decision making power so they were no longer constrained to simple instinctive response.

Sexual readiness could be conveyed and understood in a variety of ways and those with the strongest drive left the most descendants. In a couple of million years, modern humans evolved from this line of hominids and most of us inherited a relatively strong sex drive. Despite the fact that the vast majority of sexual encounters between humans are for purposes other than achieving pregnancy, human reproduction has been so successful that the world population could soon become more than the planet can support.

This inherent tendency for men to look at all women gives us at least a partial explanation of why humans are so obsessed with the female body. For instance, a typical movie features a fully clothed, dominant male and a pretty, scantily clad female. There are literally hundreds of "girlie" magazines showing nude women and almost none showing nude men. There are tens of thousands of female strippers and comparatively few male strippers. A typical female swimsuit is brief and form fitting, while males normally wear large, shapeless, boxer-short type swimwear. Female showbiz costumes show a lot of skin, leg and cleavage while men wear suits or tuxedos.

The list goes on and on but why is it so one-sided? Why is the female body the personification of sexiness? Why not the male body, or both equally? Why do so many magazines tell women how to be more beautiful, how to dress more seductively and, in general, how to appear sexier? Males certainly do appreciate the beauty of the female body but that can't be the total answer. Women appreciate the classic male body just as much, but *they have no instinct to look at men and search for visual signs of male sexual readiness.*

Looking at males has never been a requirement for species survival. Any female who survived to the age of reproduction automatically became a potential mother and it was entirely up to the males to see her signs and try to mate.

Men have this strong, primal instinct to look at women and there has been little incentive to suppress this urge. "Girl watching" has always been accepted as man's favorite pastime. Women have always been aware of this attention but they also realized that essentially all women get the same attention so they have done all they can to make themselves more alluring.

There is much more to attraction between the sexes than a few primitive instincts. Over the centuries, human females have developed and used dozens of verbal and non-verbal cues and most men have had no problem in recognizing them. Human females still retain the primitive instinctive response to mate with an alpha male but they can easily override this urge. Still, there are plenty of indications to suggest that women are sexually attracted to men in positions of power.

Since the alpha male in all other species was the biggest and strongest, women are also instinctively attracted to big, strong, healthy men in general and especially if they are the winners in some male competitive event. For the most part, though, there is enough variety in human appearance, demeanor and individual preference to insure that everyone has some quality which appeals to members of the opposite sex.

The primitive male instinct to associate red, swollen labia with sexual readiness may explain how face makeup originated. Since the beginning of the human species, men have been preferentially attracted to women with full, red lips. The men didn't know why, because instincts don't come equipped with explanations but they knew that what they saw was appealing and arousing.

Women couldn't help but notice this so the first makeup was undoubtedly some creative way to make their lips appear larger and redder. Since then, some shade of red lip coloring has been a standard part of women's makeup. It has only been in the last few years that unnatural colors such as green, blue and black lipsticks have become available. They certainly attract attention but will probably never be widely accepted because they are not inherently appealing to men.

Since the advent of cosmetic surgery, many women have also opted to increase the fullness of their lips with injections or operations. The cosmetic surgery industry has literally grown by leaps and bounds in the last few years and is increasing all the time. The customers are primarily women but the wish to be more attractive is certainly present in men, too.

More and more men are opting for cosmetic surgery as well as other enhancements such as wearing jewelry, wearing more revealing clothes, going to hair stylists and even using some types of makeup. Still, there are no big companies that specialize in male makeup. There are no giant chain stores like Fredericks of Hollywood and Victoria's Secret that sell sexy male lingerie, no male beauty salons on every block, and no magazines full of beauty tips for men.

This one-sided emphasis on female beauty and allure is universal and there are many sound arguments and rational reasons why it is necessary for women to look their best in our modern world. The origin of this tendency, however, started long before modern times and has a much simpler answer. Men are hard-wired to look at women, all women, but females have never had to look at males. For hundreds of millions of years, all a female had to do was display a certain signal, which was hormonally induced, and then reject all males that didn't measure up to her instinctive criteria.

Humans have certainly added many complications to what is, to most species, a fairly simple, instinctive interaction between the sexes. We seem to be the only species to realize there is a connection between sex and pregnancy. As far as we know, no other species is aware of the connection and the individuals are simply following their instincts. All humans learn the "facts of life" quite early but despite all of our knowledge and sophistication, it is clear that, as a species, we still respond to some very ancient callings.

The rationale in the female fashion industry is that a woman must be "in style," but why is there such a difference in male and female styles? With the exception of a few things such as neckties, men's fashions are primarily practical, functional and comfortable. Women's clothes, on the other hand, are often quite decorative but non-functional, too tight, skimpy, uncomfortable and expensive.

Men are very much responsible for this trend, of course, because they have always paid closer attention to the women who looked, acted and dressed more suggestively. However, it has been women's response to this male trait that has determined the course of the female fashion industry. If there is a demand, there will be a supply, and clearly the majority of women will do what they can, spend whatever they can afford and wear whatever it takes to accentuate their femininity and to look more alluring and sexually desirable.

In a typical United States shopping mall about half of the businesses are specialty shops that cater exclusively to women. They sell goods such as casual clothes, footwear, accessories, evening wear, bridal gowns, lingerie, wigs, and beauty products and also services such as hair styling, manicures and pedicures. Another 25%, including the big department stores, sell products for both men and women. The remaining shops are mostly assorted bookstores, eating places and such.

There might be one shop exclusively for men's suits and/or tuxedos and perhaps one dedicated to male sports gear and accessories. Men may still have the largest management role in this free market economy but women are the primary consumers.

Most men are so comfortable with the automatic tendency to scan all women that they are often not even aware of it. Many go through the motions unconsciously. They may even do it when they are with their special woman. Some women accept it as "just being a man" and feel that it's alright if all he does is look. Others feel that it is demeaning and insist that it is unacceptable and cannot continue. A woman who will not put up with this behavior is the best incentive a man can have to continually suppress this instinctive reaction.

This is not meant to imply that women do not look at men. Of course they do, but they don't spend a lot of time doing it. Women are not interested in checking out all men or even a lot of them, only the few who appeal to them. They don't study, stare and ogle, they merely glance. A quick glance can assess a whole crowd of men and eliminate them all at once or perhaps all but one or two.

Even after locating someone of interest, a woman doesn't spend a lot of time looking at him. Most feminine signals require no more than the briefest of eye contact until a dialogue is established. After that, she usually gives him her full attention and is not distracted by the presence of other men.

The traits women use to attract male attention are often referred to as "feminine wiles." Being "a flirt" or "a coquette" or "a tease" implies sexual readiness that may or may not be genuine. Often the attention and the accompanying feeling of power over men are the desired end result. Sometimes a woman may just need a male volunteer to do a task that is difficult for her and may be looking for a helper rather than a mate.

Regardless of motives, women have always been able to use these traits very effectively. This behavior must be at least partially instinctive because girls less than two years old, who have no clue about sexuality, use similar tactics all the time to wrap grown men around their little fingers.

Human females have probably been covering their genital areas since the connection between sex and pregnancy became known and they started consciously thinking of the consequences of their choice of mates. Even in tropical climates, early explorers found primitive people with coverings such as loincloths and wraps similar to diapers. Once the concept of modesty became established, removal of the covering became a definite indication of sexual readiness.

Female breasts, however, are not actually genitalia and were not covered until humans moved into colder climates and had to start fashioning clothing for warmth. Because breasts are so uniquely feminine, as soon as they were routinely hidden from view, they too came to be regarded as sexual symbols and became another area to be covered out of modesty.

Some cultures require women to wear large, shapeless robes with hoods and veils to conceal every hint of their femininity. This is truly male domination carried to the extreme. It is total control and subjugation with no logic, reason or compassion involved. Domination was discussed in the previous chapter but it is worth reiterating because there is usually a significant sexual aspect associated with male domination of women.

An extreme example is what the Taliban forced on the women of Afghanistan for several years. Every man became the master of all women. The men dealt out severe punishment or even death for any perceived infraction and felt quite justified, first because they instinctively felt it was their natural right and also because their religious leaders told them they were the absolute masters of women.

But did all that power over women make them happy? By all indications they seemed to be the angriest bunch of guys on the planet and the women surely weren't happy. What kind of quality of life is that?

The sexual aspect of this particular male-dominated culture literally implies that men are neither required nor expected to exercise any self-control in the presence of women and that if any part of a woman's body is exposed it is an open invitation to have sex. This puts the total responsibility for remaining "chaste and pure" on the woman and essentially absolves the man of any guilt even if he rapes her. This is an example of what can happen when humans blindly follow primitive instincts that clearly have no place in a civilized world.

Another is a barbaric and sometimes fatal mutilation of young girls in an attempt to remove their sexual drive. No longer common but probably still occurring in a few remote locations, the clitoris is simply cut away. The cutting instrument is normally not clean, the area is not sterile and no anesthetic is used. Days of agony follow and the chance of infection is high. The obvious intent is to keep women from "straying" by removing their center of sexual pleasure. Only the women who have survived this torture can speak of the actual effects, which, at the very least, may include years of sexual tension and frustration.

Men in positions of power and influence have convinced entire societies to adopt this incredible measure as a part of their culture. Mothers actually help hold their daughters down during this cruel ordeal. This is simply one of many examples of how men have used the vast ability of the human brain to come up with some very inhumane ways to dominate and control women.

Since all cultures of the world are largely male-dominated, sexual bondage has been, and still is, a reality for far too many disadvantaged women. In the southern United States, prior to the Civil War, an integral part of slavery was that essentially any white male had sexual access to female slaves.

Teenage sons of plantation owners regularly had sex with slaves, some of whom were probably their half-sisters. As the sons grew older and inherited the plantations, many of them, knowingly or unknowingly, had sex with their own daughters and even granddaughters. And this was all considered perfectly acceptable.

Soon there were people with more than 90% white heritage being born as slaves into this white-dominated society. The concept of "passing for white" began and raised legal questions. Finally, the Southern court system actually had to answer the preposterous question; "What percentage of black heritage made a person legally black and therefore a slave, or legally white and therefore free?" The majority of Southerners at that time considered this simply another legal problem with no moral or ethical overtones.

Of course, the whole practice of sex with slaves was a one-way street. If a white woman gave birth to a child with any discernable black features it was considered to be a mortal sin. Often the woman, the child and one or more male slaves were killed to avenge this unspeakable crime, all with no consequences for the killers. Obviously, reason and logical thinking did not enter into this picture as the men blindly followed their ancient instincts of dominance and sex drive.

Unfortunately, pockets of sexual bondage still exist even in the supposedly enlightened societies. Women and even young girls from depressed areas and poor countries are regularly lured into lives of sexual bondage. Children are often sold or rented to pedophiles.

In the United States, local sects, under the guise of the Mormon religion, practice a deplorable form of polygamy in which young girls are given to men with many "wives" as soon as they are capable of conceiving a child. Polygamy is a crime in itself, but this is also rampant pedophilia. In most cases it is known, but ignored, by local officials.

Prostitution has been around since the beginning of our species. In fact, it has been called the "world's oldest profession" and will probably be a fact of life for centuries to come. It has also been called a victimless crime because if the buyer and seller are both mentally competent, willing adults, it is difficult to justify defining either of them as the victim.

The vast majority of humans have had and, indeed still have, ample opportunities to engage in prostitution, either as a customer or a provider. Many adults have made that choice without causing harm or injury to anyone. In the big scheme of things, these encounters seem relatively unimportant but no civilized society should allow any adult to be forced into any kind of sexual behavior against their will. Even more importantly, no minor should be subject to any type of sexual exploitation under any circumstance.

Whether we wish to acknowledge it or not, there is a big demand for "sex for money" almost everywhere. Many nations around the world maintain thriving sex markets. Most big cities have at least one designated "sin area" that operates with partial or total immunity from laws and regulations. Some governments even derive income in this manner.

The majority of the prostitutes are female and a significant percentage of them have chosen the brothels but others are prisoners with no hope of escape. Hundreds of young women and girls from affluent families are abducted every year while on vacation or spring break and never heard from again.

Any female who can be sold is a potential target for abduction but some are considered more valuable than others. True blondes and redheads are relatively rare in our species as a whole and tend to bring the highest prices especially if they are young and shapely.

If these poor, unfortunate girls develop recognizable signs of a serious disease, they become instant liabilities. Since freeing them would risk exposing the whole sinister operation, most are simply killed and their bodies disposed of where they will never be found. Those who profit from this sexual slavery regard the girls as expendable commodities to be discarded when they are no longer a viable source of income.

Humans in general have strong sex drives. Various forms of self-stimulation are often used by both sexes for temporary relief of sexual tension but most people strongly prefer sexual interactions with a partner. Even in very repressive societies and other situations where men and women are kept isolated from each other, sexual activity goes on unabated. In institutions such as prisons, same-sex encounters are very common even though the percentage of prisoners who are true homosexuals may be quite small. Many of the encounters are between consenting adults but in any type of power struggle, sex is often used as a manifestation of dominance.

A high percentage of criminals, especially violent ones, are driven to dominate anyone they can and the number of people one can force to submit sexually is a clear indicator of a high position in a dominance hierarchy. Prison inmates are usually quite overt and blatant about their acts of dominance while others, such as pedophiles, normally must be very covert and sneaky but they all have one thing in common; the driving need to dominate and use other humans.

One obvious aspect of being an alpha or other high-ranking male of any species is having sexual access to many females. An integral part of alpha status is the instinctive drive to deny that access to other males. In most species this is accomplished, or at least attempted, by brute strength and intimidation of both subordinate males and females.

Especially since the advent of civilization, human males have tried to expand that control by making laws and rules aimed at limiting female sexual activity. There is no evidence to suggest that any of these rules and laws were originated by women.

In repressive societies women have little or no choice but to obey whatever is decreed by the men in charge but even in cultures with more freedoms, most women accept the restrictions, at least in principle, especially if they apply to both sexes. Possessiveness, jealousy and even aggression, though at a more covert level, can be equally as strong in women as in men.

Since domination and sex drive are human instincts rather than strictly male, it follows that if women were the dominant sex and were responsible for formulating our moral rules, there is no reason to believe that they would be significantly different than those that currently exist in open societies.

There would probably be much less violence and bloodshed in a female-dominated world because women are not subject to the supercharging effects of testosterone but as far as sexual activity is concerned, there might not be much difference. History shows that women who have achieved positions of absolute power have had their own versions of harems, consorts and liaisons commonly associated with male rulers.

Living in relatively small, competitive groups has been the predominant way of life for essentially all species for the past billion years. It just turned out to be the best way to produce more and better offspring. However, there were two potentially serious problems concerning sexual behavior that had to be worked out very early.

First, in any small group, there is the possibility of incest, which can ruin a gene pool in a few generations. Females have always known their male offspring and long ago developed a strong instinct against mating with them even if they became alpha males. For the most part, they probably recognized their brothers also and rejected them.

On the other hand, males of most species had no clue about parental relationships and so did not know who their female offspring were. No doubt, some father-daughter mating occurred in some of the larger groups but it was not the norm because the dominance hierarchy frequently changed. The alpha and any other high-ranking males who actually got to breed were regularly displaced by the young males working their way up. This continual supply of new breeding males essentially reduced father-daughter incest to a negligible level.

The other problem concerned interaction between neighboring groups, which consisted mostly of fighting. When a random mutation would occasionally give an individual some type of advantage in the struggle for dominance, that individual normally became a breeding male and the trait quickly spread throughout the group. If there were no interbreeding between groups the advantage would not be shared with the rest of the species.

Fortunately, there has always been clandestine mating between members of rival groups no matter how intense the rivalry. Both males and females, primarily the young adults, had strong urges to stray into neighboring territories despite the dangers of trespassing.

Sometimes they were attacked and driven off or even killed but often they found attractive strangers who wanted to make love, not war. There was enough interbreeding in this manner to spread any advantageous characteristic throughout the entire species within a few generations.

This tendency to stray into "enemy territory" and have forbidden sex with attractive strangers is common in humans also. We have a long history of marriages and clandestine mating with members of other races, religions, cultures, etc. even when strictly forbidden.

From family feuds like the Hatfields and McCoys to nations at war, there has always been both overt and covert fraternization with the "enemy." Sexual attraction between individuals is determined by many factors and man-made taboos do nothing to diminish this attraction. In fact, they may even cause the "forbidden fruit" syndrome and actually enhance the allure of what they are meant to prevent.

Recent research has shown that strong physical attraction between two people results in a physiological release of chemicals that is responsible for symptoms such as increased pulse rate, shortness of breath, nervousness, excitement and sexual stimulation. Increased levels of dopamine and adrenalin have been found in both men and women experiencing high levels of attraction. The feeling is certainly enhanced when the attraction is mutual but it can be, and often is, completely one-sided.

Ideally, when two people meet and experience these wonderful feelings they find that they are well suited for each other and ultimately get married. If all, or at least most other factors are positive, the feelings of excitement can reoccur time and time again for up to a year or sometimes even longer, but then they tend to disappear. By that time, compatible couples have had time to develop strong bonds that often lead to lasting love relationships. Long term, true love relationships can develop without this initial heart-flutter phase if the couple stays together for other reasons until the strong bonds have had time to form.

This heady, excited, rapturous feeling has been interpreted by humans as a basis for our concept of "romantic love." It has been eloquently described by songwriters, poets and novelists the world over. Roberta Flack gave us one of the more poignant and emotional interpretations with her beautiful rendition of Ewan MacColl's classic love song: "The First Time Ever."

> The first time ever I saw your face
> I thought the sun rose in your eyes
> And the moon and stars were the gifts you gave
> To the dark and the endless skies

The chemical release can be triggered by any or all of our primary senses; sight, sound and scent. The feeling may be described as "a crush," "puppy love," "infatuation," "physical attraction," "love at first sight," or similar terms. No matter what it is called, it is an effective inducement to bring males and females together and typically leads to mating.

The sex drive is definitely a part of this feeling but anyone can feel sexual tension and arousal without the other symptoms. Countless teenage girls and young women with their hearts aflutter have given themselves to hormonally charged young men who are feeling nothing but the sex drive. Some women also have been known to take advantage of "love struck" young men simply for release of their sexual tension.

Most of us believe that this syndrome is unique to humans but the chemical release is probably common to at least all mammal species. Elevated levels of dopamine and adrenalin have been detected in female lab rats when exposed to alpha males during their mating cycle. The reaction is entirely involuntary and therefore must be instinctive rather than the result of conscious decision.

Lovemaking seems especially urgent during this initial phase of attraction and, at least for the first few weeks or even months, requires little or no foreplay. An old adage that has been around for many years says; "If you put a penny in a large jar every time you make love during the first year of your marriage and take a penny out each time after that, you will never empty the jar." While this is not literally true for all marriages, it is a fairly accurate assessment of the exhilarating feeling that is so common when love is "new."

In countries where people have freedom of choice when it comes to choosing their mates and dates, most relationships probably start out with this exciting phase. Like a line from another popular song by Rod Stewart;

I really must admit right now, the attraction was purely physical.

This intense attraction generally conjures up all manner of positive assumptions about the object of our affection. The assumptions are normally based on very little solid information and are essentially the product of looking at the person through the proverbial "rose-colored glasses."

Often many or all of the rosy assumptions are found to be false when the true personality of the individual is revealed. Nothing kills the thrill of initial attraction faster than the recognition of negative attributes such as rage, intense jealousy, possessiveness, need for control, cruelty or infidelity. Some of these negative personal traits may take longer to surface than others but when they do become evident, the "romantic love" phase is the first casualty.

Regardless of how long this phase lasts, it will go away. When it does, if a mature love relationship has not developed the union is normally doomed. If a couple stays together for financial or other such reasons, the relationship may drift into a grudging acceptance or a strained tolerance.

Couples who fail to develop mature love bonds often opt for divorce once the romantic love dies out. It may be referred to as "falling out of love," "outgrowing one's mate," "incompatibility" or simply "drifting apart." Whatever the terminology, one or both partners begin to feel disappointed, disillusioned and trapped. First marriages are especially vulnerable to this fate since they are often based on little more than physical attraction and wishful thinking. Those who "get it right the first time" are quite fortunate whether they realize it or not.

Most people who find themselves in a failing marriage soon meet someone new who reactivates the initial excitement response. This normally hastens the divorce or leads to infidelity or both. Some people seem almost addicted to this feeling to the point that they cannot develop a lasting relationship and they move on to someone new as soon as the infatuation begins to wane.

Physical attraction is basically an involuntary response and it is certainly an important part of any relationship but it is only one of many aspects of long-term compatibility. Factors of perhaps even greater importance such as trust, honesty, fidelity, consideration, equality, openness, common goals and interests and others are primarily the result of conscious decisions, which are higher brain functions. The versatility and individuality made possible by our magnificent brains actually makes it difficult for us to find the right mate.

In the course of a week or a month, most of us see several people who appear attractive to us. It's easy to get the idea that there are many suitable mates out there but that is not actually true. Let's face it, most people are incompatible with most other people. Just think of all the people you have been involved with in any type of relationship from casual dating to marriage. How many of these relationships turned out to be right for both of you for the long term?

If you can truthfully say that you found one person who is or was a "soul mate," you are one of a lucky minority who has gotten it right or perhaps a grieving widow or widower who has lost your "one true love." There are relatively few people who have found a second "just right" person after the untimely death of the first.

The majority of us want to find a "soul mate." Millions of single people as well as some married ones are out there looking for that special person. A significant percentage will never find anyone whom they consider to be "just right" and many of them will settle for someone who is "acceptable." With so much inherent variation in humans, there is almost certainly a "Mr Right" or "Ms Right" somewhere out there for any particular individual but even in a mobile society, the odds of meeting that person are actually quite low.

Population statistics tell us that there are more women in the world than men. Given the higher mortality rate among males, this should be no surprise. Somewhere in the late teens or early twenties age brackets, the numbers are approximately equal but by the late twenties, women start to outnumber men. The ratio becomes more one-sided with each passing year. Factors other than sheer numbers also affect this ratio. World-wide there are about twice as many gay men as lesbians and there are more than ten times as many men in prisons as women. Given the dismal success rate of first marriages and the fact that compatibility is relatively rare, the bottom line is that for most of a woman's adult life, her chances of finding a suitable mate are significantly lower than those of her male counterparts.

CHAPTER 7

Dominant Behavior

In the last 50 years, there have been numerous long-term studies of various species in their native habitat. Dedicated anthropologists, such as Jane Goodall, have literally made careers out of living in close contact with a particular group and meticulously observing and recording their habits. These accounts have shown remarkably similar behavior patterns regardless of the species. Since members of these species have little or no ability to reason and make decisions, their behavior is clearly instinctive. The studies are all available on the Internet and in most libraries for anyone interested in learning about instinctive behavior.

Many of the behavior patterns documented in these studies can also be recognized in typical large-scale human behavior. Many can be recognized in individual actions, even our own.

Some people spend a lot of time feeling guilty for having what they feel are evil thoughts. Most of us have wished for revenge such as wanting to hurt, maim or even kill someone, perhaps by running them over with a car. Some of us may have wished for a rich friend or close relative to die and leave us enough money for a life of luxury and power that riches can provide. Some people may be sexually attracted to their best friends mate or some other forbidden person.

These and dozens of other unwelcome thoughts that pop into our minds can cause us to agonize about our "dark side." If we know where these urges originate and why they exist we can put our minds at ease. Then the only time our conscience will bother us is if we actually make the decision to give in to an urge that we know will cause another person harm or pain.

In general, any reflex or instantaneous reaction that happens automatically, before we can think, is instinctive. As thinking humans, we all have the wonderful ability to decide which instinctive feelings are no longer appropriate in our civilized world and take justifiable pride in our ability to simply ignore or overcome them.

Perhaps the instinct that we have to deal with most often is dominance and submission. Every day we are confronted with issues of power and control at all levels. It is so much a part of our lives that we just accept it without thinking.

We all have "hot buttons." When someone pushes one of our "buttons," we feel an instantaneous flash of anger. It may be any intensity from rage to irritation but it is not something we decide to feel. It is an instinctive response. We immediately feel that someone is unjustly exerting some kind of power or control over us, looking down on us, mocking us, laughing at us or perhaps implying that we are stupid or not worthy of common courtesy.

We may perceive this behavior as a threat, an order, an insult or a putdown, but whatever it is, we feel the urge to force that person to stop. But, just stopping is not enough. We want them to actually feel regret or even fear, to take it all back and to show proper respect. In other words, we want them to be submissive.

Sometimes we are successful. We may be bigger, stronger, more threatening or a better bluffer. We may be able to mention a powerful ally who can be summoned. We may just be more articulate and enlighten the person with logic. We may be aware of the other persons "hot buttons" and turn the whole thing around so we can laugh at them. We may just decide that they are not worthy of a response and simply shrug it off and leave.

At other times, we have to be submissive. We may be forced to do something we don't want to do, verbally agree with something we know is not right, accept an insult silently or with a smile. Some situations may even require an obvious display of humility. Being submissive is normally not pleasant, but we've all done it. All humans who ever lived have done it.

Why do all groups have rulers or leaders? Why are there chiefs, warlords, drug lords, dictators, tsars, ayatollahs, monarchs, kings, premiers, presidents, earls, dukes, chancellors, pharaohs, moguls, sheiks, emirs, caliphs, khans, emperors, kaisers, dons, etc? And why are they essentially all men? They are simply the human versions of the alpha male at the top of some type of dominance hierarchy, which is common to all species.

If you think about it, it becomes obvious that the whole structure of all human society is composed of dominance hierarchies. All facets of our civilization from government and industry to social organizations, family groups, and churches are built around them. For instance, why do we need bosses at work? If the workers know what must be done, why can't they just do it without supervision? Surely a team of equals should be able to do any job. If they don't know what to do or how to do it, someone with the necessary expertise could be added to the team and provide the training. Paid consultants could also provide direction and training.

Still, most of us would be lost without a boss. Some of us would do little or nothing if we had no boss to tell us what to do and monitor our progress. We expect to have a boss. We've always had a boss, sometimes several bosses. Many of us aspire to be a boss in some capacity so that we can be the one to tell others what to do.

Everyone who has a job is aware that most people in any workplace are competing to gain positions that provide them with more authority. To many, the job itself is the most important factor, but to others, the focus of doing a good job is secondary to the quest for more power and control. These are the people most likely to abuse whatever authority they have. Soliciting and accepting bribes, sexual harassment, coercion, rape and pedophilia are common abuses of power.

Basically, any type of discrimination is also a manifestation of dominance. If we can find a reason to look down on a group or an individual it makes us feel that we are above them. The reason does not have to make sense or even be logical as long as it sounds good to us. Many people have looked at, and treated, entire races as "animals," "inferior" or "subhuman." This is completely illogical. Granted, we are all individuals. No two people are exactly alike but we are all one species.

What defines a species? It is when two members of the opposite sex can mate and have viable (fertile) offspring. Any human from anywhere in the world can potentially mate with any other human and have normal children.

In the past, populations of several continents have been isolated long enough to develop enough superficial differences to be classified as separate races, but not nearly long enough to become a separate species. 99.9% of our genes are identical to every other human being. Just 0.1% of our genetic material accounts for all of our physical and physiological differences and yet, despite education, laws and religion, racism is still common in most areas of the world.

Race is often used as a cause by hate groups. Racial differences such as skin color are easy to see and easy to focus on, but Jewish people and homosexuals are often singled out as targets also, especially by neo-nazi groups. The primary motivation for these groups is the feeling of power and control they get from being "superior to" all those "inferior" people. Some may even commit acts of violence on innocent victims to reinforce their feelings of dominance.

These individuals are also satisfying another primal instinct by belonging to a relatively small, homogenous group of individuals with similar ideas and goals; people who think the "right" way. The members are often unattractive, socially inept, undereducated and ignorant but their cause gives them something to be very proud of because, in their estimation, it elevates their status above an entire race or some other sizeable group of people.

Most members of groups that promote well-meaning but controversial causes are sincere people who really believe in the cause. Examples are the people in the "Right to Life" movement who take positive actions such as volunteering in Family Planning areas, distributing information and methods of birth control, raising funds for women's shelters and medical care, working with adoptions agencies and the like.

Unfortunately there are others who concentrate on negative actions such as bombing clinics, killing doctors and threatening unfortunate women because to them, the most important thing is to dominate, to inflict pain and force others to do their will.

In a homogeneous society with no obvious differences in race, religion or culture, other factors are used to establish position in the social hierarchy. One example is the caste system that exists in India. It is slowly changing but for centuries the majority of people in that country bought into a culture that sanctioned putting a sizeable number of their citizens in a class so low they are called "untouchables."

Most of the Indian people may not be considered the "elite" of their society but they can always look down on at least one group. It took a deep-thinking humanitarian named Gandhi to start the change. Any cultural change is met with resistance but those based on primitive instincts are especially entrenched because they feel so natural.

The primary difference between typical human dominance hierarchies and those of other species is that all other species still establish their rankings by contests of strength and bravery. Humans no longer rely on physical strength to achieve higher social status or get promoted to higher positions. Most areas of business, government and religions use positive criteria such as wisdom, intelligence, seniority, skill and leadership ability. Unfortunately, negative methods such as ruthlessness, coercion, blackmail, bribery and even murder have been used successfully by many people to move up to higher positions.

Why have humans always had rulers? Prior to civilization, we lived in small groups headed by alpha males much like all other species. At the dawn of civilization, the groups became larger and the leaders were elevated to the status of royalty. Even today, some countries still have royal families.

Actually, there is nothing royal about them except for their title, which was bestowed on them by other humans. They are mentally, physically and physiologically just like the rest of us. There is no such thing as "royal blood," "the divine right of kings" or any other distinction that sets them apart from everyone else. Any titles, descriptions or privileges they may claim are granted by people, not God.

The founding fathers of the United States certainly weren't perfect but they did see a lot of things very objectively. They clearly realized that the things they wanted for themselves such as liberty, equality, opportunity and freedom of religion were exactly what all people wanted.

The official government documents, such as the Emancipation Proclamation and later the U.S. Constitution were written with that in mind. Despite the fact that, at the time, the writers were thinking only of the interests of white men, the words were such that women and people of color could not be excluded. Eventually the U.S. legal system was able to sort it out and ensure that all freedoms apply to all citizens.

Another farsighted concept that the founders insisted on was separation of church and state. Being educated in world history, they knew that there has never been a government controlled by a single religion that has advocated true religious freedom. Unfortunately, just because people are religious does not mean they are tolerant of other religions. After all, we are only human and we instinctively want other people to see things our way; the "right" way. Historically, the religion of the ruler, or the ruling party, tended to become the "official" religion and persecution inevitably followed.

Many of the pilgrims who came to the "new world" were seeking religious freedom. Back then, religious persecution was rampant all over Europe. The new settlers immediately built churches and started practicing the religion of their choice. Being human, many of those who rose to positions of authority began discriminating against people of other religions and persecution quickly became an ugly fact of life in the colonies.

The progressive countries that have maintained separation of church and state have actually achieved a real measure of religious freedom. Until the majority of people in any country become openly tolerant, that separation must continue to be the law in order to guarantee all citizens true freedom of religion. If you have any doubts, check out the extent of religious freedom in any past or present theocracy such as an Islamic republic.

There are more Muslims in the world than any other religion, but they certainly are not united nor do they all believe the same way. There are Sunnis, Shiites, and Kurds just to name a few. Not only do they not agree, they actually have wars with each other and kill fellow Muslims. Is this really what Allah intended or are there some human emotions and decisions here?

Christians are perhaps the next largest group, but how much agreement exists among them? Most of the combatants in the European theaters of both world wars were Christians. The primary split in Christianity is between the Protestants and the Catholics, but it doesn't stop there. How many Protestant religions and sects are there and why are there so many?

Maybe all this diversity is just a result of our amazing ability to think, to imagine endless possibilities and to make decisions combined with our primal instinct to belong to a small, homogenous group of people who think the way we do, the "right" way.

Most religions are essentially dominated by males but those that have been established the longest such as Greek Orthodox, Judaism, Islam and Catholicism are the least likely to have females in any position of authority. The Catholic Church is undoubtedly the most successful at maintaining a unified following.

After the Protestants split off a few hundred years ago, the Catholic Church has remained very much a large, cohesive, well-organized unit. There is often some minor local dissension among the rank and file, but no serious attempts to break away from the mainstream. No other religion has an international governing body like the Vatican and none get as much publicity or are as familiar to the average person.

There are many classic examples of successful male dominance hierarchies in the world but, because of all the publicity, none are as well known as the Catholic Church. The Pope is the Alpha, the Cardinals are the Betas and so on down to the Priests, who occupy the lowest male positions, and below them are the nuns. Some of the males are content with their positions and some are working their way up, aspiring to someday be the alpha. All show appropriate deference to those in higher positions and gracious but perhaps occasionally condescending behavior to those beneath them.

Religions all over the world have always provided many positions of leadership and authority for those who feel the need to spread the word of their deity. Almost without exception, these are people who are convinced that they have somehow been blessed with the knowledge of the truth about God and the way to Salvation. They also feel the need to share this knowledge with others.

Many, such as Billy Graham, are true proponents of religious freedom. They live exemplary lives and dedicate themselves to the peaceful pursuit of enlightening others who may not be as sure of their faith. Most leaders associated with the major religions in developed countries seem to agree with this philosophy.

Unfortunately, a significant percentage of religious leaders around the world have no tolerance for religious freedom. These are usually extremely dominant men with a driving need to control others. For them it is not enough to live their own lives in accordance with their beliefs. They feel that everyone should be forced to accept and observe their version of "the one true way."

Instead of peaceful persuasion these leaders may use their influence to incite the more volatile members of their following to use coercion, threats and violence to stamp out any opposition and achieve total obedience. The most extreme want nothing less than to be the head of a religious dictatorship or at least the primary religious influence in a military dictatorship. The late Ayatollah Khomeni is an example of this type.

The fact that most other religious leaders in the world do not agree with them seems to be totally irrelevant. Obviously, anyone who disagrees is wrong! What could be more "right' than the "true word of God?" It is actually quite easy for individuals to justify religious zeal and even fanaticism because their cause is so holy, so divine and so right. They are totally convinced that they alone know the truth and to them, "enlightenment" is basically "obey or else."

There are leaders, such as some Islamic Mullahs and Ayatollahs, who even view other leaders in the same religion who have some different practices or beliefs as dangerous adversaries rather than just misguided unfortunates. If the drive to become and remain an alpha male is strong enough, it can override all reason, logic and tolerance in some individuals, even religious leaders. They will use all available means and all possible tactics to force challengers into submission.

With all these varying viewpoints, the big question is "Who is right?" We can't all be right. Most individuals like to feel that they are members of a relatively small group that has found the right path. But who among us, leader or follower, is privy to the actual word and will of God? Who has sorted through the countless beliefs, arguments, texts and stories and correctly determined where the word of God ends and the word of man begins? Could it be that all this variation is simply because we have large brains capable of deep, abstract thinking and we are able to imagine endless possibilities?

There are so many conflicting details and requirements from one religion to another and even between divisions of the same religion that we can only come to one logical conclusion. Many, perhaps most, of the ideas and practices that are put forth as requirements of God must actually be man-made rules.

We humans have always been prone to making false assumptions and coming to erroneous conclusions. In the absence of definitive proof, our minds fill in the unknowns with all manner of conjecture, wishful thinking and hearsay. Myths, legends and questionable versions of history are clear examples of this human trait and yet the majority of humans feel that their own personal beliefs and practices are right and that all people who think differently are wrong. Many also believe that the "truth" is so obvious that all those mistaken and misguided people should be able to easily see it.

How can we, on one hand, profess that church doctrine is the word of God and at the same time disagree with all other established religions and even with some parts our own religion? For example, literally millions of devout Catholics get divorced, practice birth control, have sex outside of marriage, feel that priests should be allowed to marry and feel that women should be allowed to be priests. These views are in direct opposition to the rules that come directly from the Vatican. This behavior is by no means unique to Catholics as it is common to all religions.

How can this be? No religious person would actually disagree with the word of God. The only possible answer is that most people believe that some of the doctrine and teachings of all religions are man-made rules and not the word of God. This seems to be a reasonable assumption since history is full of examples of beliefs that have subsequently been proven false.

In the early 1600s, soon after it was discovered that the earth and other planets revolved around our sun, an Italian named Giordano Bruno went a step farther and said that there were planets orbiting other stars as well. He was accused of being a heretic and when he wouldn't recant, he was burned at the stake. Modern astronomers have proven that many, perhaps most, stars have one or more planets in orbit around them, so Bruno was correct.

We don't know why Bruno was so convinced that he would rather die a horrible death than simply say he was wrong because there was not a shred of evidence to support his claim at the time. He was an intensely religious man so perhaps he felt that God had told him. Many people feel that God has come to them in dreams and visions and such, but most likely, God has communicated directly with very few of us. Since Bruno was right, perhaps he was, indeed, one of the few that God has actually spoken to. We will never know but it certainly makes more sense than assuming that God directed the people who made the decision to burn him at the stake.

So what is the answer? Since we can't all be right, maybe none of us are completely right. Unfortunately, we humans instinctively want to be members of an elite group who are "right" while everyone else is wrong. Moreover, we actually prefer that our group is relatively small. We do not want to be just another anonymous face in a sea of literally billions of people who all believe the same way.

Whether we accept the religion that we grew up with or adopt a different one later on that seems to suit us better, we do so because we want our viewpoint to be the "right" one. If we are part of the "right" religion, it means that we are members of the "in group," the chosen few who are eligible for heaven and eternal life. There appears to be some self-deception here. It suggests that we feel we are in some way smarter or more perceptive than all those other misguided people who really ought to know better but just haven't quite grasped the big picture.

If we think critically about this idea, we can only conclude that it makes no sense at all that so many people could be wrong while only our group is right. At least in the open societies of the world, everyone has access to the same writings and teachings. Despite all our wishful thinking, if there were truly only one "right way" why haven't the majority of us seen it? Why are there so many different religions, sects and splinter groups?

Is it really reasonable that God would actually forsake billions of otherwise faithful, religious people simply because they practice religions that are different from ours? That seems highly unlikely, perhaps even preposterous. It suggests that we are assuming that God has human emotions, frailties and limitations. Logically it makes much more sense that God doesn't care what religion we belong to and if this is true, why do we care? Why is it so important to us? Perhaps it is because we have human emotions, frailties and limitations.

Three of the world's major religions, Islam, Judaism and Christianity, trace their lineage back through one man, Abraham. All three view him as the patriarch of monotheism, which was a somewhat radical concept at the time. This brings up what seems to be a painfully obvious question. If Abraham believed in God, was faithful to God and, within the bounds of human frailty, led an exemplary life, what more is required of anyone?

By all accounts, God communicated with Abraham but none of these accounts even hint that God told him that he or his descendants would start three separate religions with dozens of divisions and breakaway sects and a host of different belief systems in each. Abraham himself had no specific name for his religious beliefs so why do we have so many different names and labels specifying our particular system? Why do we have so many major and minor variations on the same simple ideology?

Logically, it is just not realistic to assume that God has led so many different people in so many different directions. More reasonably, because of the versatility of our large brains, many humans have injected their own unique ideas, illusions and vagaries into what should be the uncomplicated theology of Abraham. This makes it virtually impossible for us to separate the few mandatory rules that Abraham lived by from the massive tangle of man-made rules and requirements that humans have insisted on. We are all susceptible to this way of thinking because we all have the large brains plus the instinct to belong to the "right" group.

Regardless of how "right" we feel we are, maybe we don't have to be identified with a certain religion that happens to appeal to our way of thinking. Maybe God doesn't require the pomp and ceremony, the rituals, the specific rules of conduct, the ornate churches and dozens of other details, minutia and trappings that we humans insist on. Perhaps all we need is faith and an earnest resolve to be a good person. Not just a good neighbor, family member, patriot, worker, church-goer or any other single virtue but an all around good person who strives to help build a society based on tolerance, moderation, kindness, peace and brotherly love. Everyone who is not mentally impaired has the ability to make that choice.

CHAPTER 8

Group Living

Prior to civilization, like all other species, our ancestors lived in relatively small groups. They were our clan, our tribe, our friends, our "people" and everyone else was a stranger and a potential enemy. Modern humans are still very group-oriented. We instinctively want to belong to a group of familiar, trustworthy, likeminded people.

We are most comfortable in a group that is large enough so that we have the safety of numbers and small enough so that everybody knows everybody else. And we feel the need for a leader to provide organization, direction, meaning and security. The vast majority of us do not function quite as well without a leader.

If you think about it, it becomes quite clear that essentially all groups are dominance hierarchies. We long to know where we fit into the group structure, our "place" so to speak. As a rule, we tend to be uncomfortable around leaderless groups. They seem too much like unruly mobs, directionless and unpredictable, maybe even a little scary.

Since the advent of civilization, our groups have gotten larger and more numerous. Most of us belong to several groups such as fraternal organizations, lodges, sports clubs, fan clubs, neighborhood watches, churches, professional groups, hobby clubs etc. And we often pay dues for the privilege of being a member.

New groups are constantly being formed and the first thing a group has to have is a leader. If no one steps up to assume that role, we elect one and often several other positions under the leader. Some of us want to be leaders and others just want to be members, however, as soon as the boss starts laying down some rules, inevitably someone will disagree. It may or may not be a serious challenge but because of human nature there will always some degree of dissension within groups.

Businesses are natural dominance hierarchies usually headed by an alpha male although many women also operate businesses. Many bosses are kind, benevolent, even compassionate people who realize the importance of the workers and take care of them. At the other extreme are those who exploit workers as much as possible and begrudge every penny that comes out of the profits. It was this extreme that gave rise to labor unions. A typical relationship between management and labor has to be described as adversarial rather than cooperative. It is a power struggle that has led to substantial benefits for many workers along with some less positive outcomes.

Unfortunately, unions are just groups of humans and they also become dominance hierarchies. Union bosses and stewards have used their power and influence for personal gain. Serious graft and corruption have been uncovered, especially in the larger organizations. Some unions have even felt so powerful that their demands have led to their own downfall.

Examples are unions that caused movie studios to close or leave the United States, railroad unions guilty of blatant "featherbedding" and the FAA Air Traffic Controllers union members who went on strike and were fired. The Air Traffic controllers actually felt that they were so powerful and so important because of the nature of their work that they could bring the US government to its knees. Few people had any sympathy when they heard the union's excessive demands.

Blindly following primitive instincts to climb to the top with no regard for anyone else has led to many new millionaires. Does any society really need more millionaires? Does any person really need to be a millionaire? If we are comfortable and secure, do we really need more? Of course the answer is NO, but we want more. The majority of humans want more no matter how much they already have. Wealth means power and power means control over more people and control means alpha status.

Anyone who is familiar with North and South America can see that people from many different countries and cultures can live together in peace. For instance, the vast majority of the inhabitants of the United States consider themselves Americans first and their other heritage second. People from all ethnic origins fought as American patriots in the World Wars, many against the countries of their ancestry. There is room and opportunity for all who are here and more who are coming.

In retrospect, there was obviously plenty of room for the Europeans when they first came to settle in the "New World." So, the question is: Was all the fighting, bloodshed, misery and death really necessary? Unfortunately, at that time it was inevitable. No group gives up the territory they claim as their homeland without a fight. The "New World" was already populated by groups of Native Americans and even though there was a lot of open land, there was no unclaimed territory.

Once the Europeans moved in and started settling the open land, there was no longer enough room for the Native American way of life. That way of life was essentially the same as our ancestors had lived for hundreds of thousands of years.

For centuries before the Europeans came, both North and South America were inhabited by literally thousands of separate groups. As time went by, advances in agriculture, metallurgy and architecture allowed for larger and larger groups but despite significant trade, technology transfer and interbreeding, the groups remained as autonomous tribal units.

Each tribe had it's own language, culture and customs and considered all other tribes as enemies. There were numerous short-term alliances for purposes such as defense and invasion but no long-term merging, no common language except sign language and no large-scale cooperation for the common good. This behavior is not unique and should not be surprising because it is completely natural. It is what all species do.

Because of their superior weapons, the Europeans definitely had an advantage but on numerous occasions their single-shot firearms made little or no difference against larger numbers. For many years the settlers were completely at the mercy of the native tribes but because of long-standing rivalries, many tribes preferred to side with the newcomers rather than their old "enemies."

It was this lack of unity among the tribes, this wholesale inability to override ancient instincts that sealed their fate. Like countless other societies before and since, they were conquered and had to adapt to the invader's way of life. The cultures, territories and ways that were important enough to die for were lost forever because of their resistance to come together as one united nation.

The descendants of those original tribes have integrated into the new societies but it has been a long and painful process. Those who have kept some degree of tribal integrity and identity have done so through the legal systems of the democracies that they are part of. Many have held on to bits and pieces of their old cultures out of pride and fond remembrance of their ancestral heritage but no one actually has any illusions about returning to the "old days and old ways" in this modern age.

Literally billions of humans have died painful, premature deaths fighting for and against similar lost causes and for what? For "our way of life," what else? Is there a lesson we can learn here?

When our modern human ancestors started migrating out of Africa around eighty thousand years ago, they settled all of habitable areas they came to starting in southern Asia. Some groups were able to stay in their new lands and others had to move on as their numbers grew ever larger. At first they moved primarily to the south populating all of Indonesia and Malaysia and in a few thousand years they had reached Australia. Later when the climate became more favorable they spread farther north and by forty thousand years ago they inhabited all of Asia and Europe.

About twenty thousand years ago the first groups of our ancestors were able to move across the land bridge into the Americas during an extended period when mean sea level was exceptionally low. About 12,000 years ago, the bridge opened again and more people made their way across. The Europeans who first discovered the "New World" had no idea that they shared a common heritage with the Native Americans.

Until recently, few people realized that all humans share a common ancestry. In the last fifteen to twenty years, a massive effort in tracking mitochondrial DNA has confirmed that all modern humans are descendants of the same group that originated in Africa one hundred to two hundred thousand years ago.

Soon we humans, as a species, need a reality check. Millions of us are already aware and are genuinely concerned. Millions more don't care and billions of us have no way of knowing but we need to realize that this planet is the only home we have and it needs much more care and preventative maintenance that it is currently getting. Blind adherence to outmoded instincts will undoubtedly damage our beautiful home, perhaps to the point of destruction.

Science has shown us that our world is simply a large, self-contained space ship in orbit around one of the stars in our galaxy. We have enough food, water, clean air and other supplies for now but our natural resources are finite and we are using them up at an alarming rate. We all want a good life for our children and grandchildren but without some better estate planning, will there be anything left for any of our descendants?

We all have to realize that our "territory," our "homeland" is not a certain city, state or nation, it is the planet Earth. Our "group" is not our clan, our tribe, our church, our race, our culture or any other superficial classification. Our group is the entire human race.

We are no longer just another species struggling to survive. We have populated the world and altered it to suit our needs. Our technology is so awesome it could actually be used to destroy us along with countless other species. We could literally bring an end to the "Age of Mammals" and open the whole world up to insects and microbes.

The only way to ensure a safe, secure life for our descendants is to make the world safe and secure for all those who are already here. With the destructive tendencies of "human nature" how can this be done? It seems so simple. If all governments stopped declaring war on other countries and waged all out war on the criminals and predators within their own societies, the battle would be almost won. Some cooperation, sharing of resources, quality education and birth control would take care of the rest. If only . . . .

When astronauts get their first view of Earth from space, the first thing that strikes them is the awesome beauty of our planet. The second realization for many of them is that, except for shorelines, there are no visible national boundaries. The man-made lines so prominent on globes and maps and in legal systems are not really there. They are self-imposed dividing lines that are meant to keep people apart. Isn't it about time we quit drawing those lines and start trying to erase some of them so we can work together for the preservation of our world?

There are ample indications that millions of people want more cooperation and unity and less dissension. All the progressive countries of the world have become virtual melting pots for all races and cultures. Even countries such as Japan that for centuries have been almost obsessive about maintaining "racial purity" are becoming more and more tolerant of racial mixing.

The European countries that created a common market system and adopted a common currency are taking positive steps toward the concept of nations working together instead of insisting on "our way only." The next logical step of adopting a common language would set the stage for national mergers at some time in the future. As yet there has been no serious attempt to discuss mergers but what an awesome step that would be toward erasing some of those dividing lines.

There are definitely places where it would be much easier to start such a radical trend as merging instead of more separating. For instance, in the United States, why do we have fifty states? Why are there two Dakotas, two Virginias and two Carolinas? Those six states could set a tremendous precedent by merging into three states, Dakota, Virginia and Carolina. After the details were ironed out and the benefits became evident more states might follow. In fact why do we have any state smaller than say Texas, or even Alaska. Those two seem to do just fine.

Eventually we might decide that we do not need state boundaries and just become one solid country with no state rivalries. Canada and Mexico might even do the same thing and at some point might even want to join us in forming the nation of North America. This may seem like a fantasy but before too much longer, our species needs to get rid of separatism in favor of togetherness or the majority of humans face a grim future.

CHAPTER 9

Individuals

The related fields of Psychology and Psychiatry have struggled for centuries to explain human behavior, both individual and group, and to find some sort of help or treatment for those with "behavioral problems." It has become increasingly apparent that there are no simple explanations; no easy solutions. Individual human behavior can be loosely described as how a person reacts to his or her total environment. This depends on a host of variables. Every conceivable facet of our lives from the moment of birth has some effect on the way we think and act.

Factors that influence our behavior go back even farther than the time of our birth. We are also strongly impacted by our genetic makeup. We are not actually born as "blank slates" because some of our physiology and, therefore, parts of our future personality have already been established. Despite our similarities, each person is unique and not exactly like anyone else. Even identical twins have many small differences.

The moment of conception determines the specific DNA that we inherit which is a combination of our parent's DNA, but every ovule in our mother's body is ever so slightly different from the rest as are all the sperm cells produced by our father. In turn, our parent's DNA is a product of countless generations of our ancestors.

After that instant of fertilization there are a myriad of minute differences in fetal development and birthing that have varying effects on the physiology of the growing brain and body of the baby. Every woman's body is slightly different and the countless interactions between the mother's body and the fetus are all affected to some degree by hundreds of external as well as internal vagaries. Because of all these factors, plus the enormous capacity of the human brain to perceive and imagine, each individual will react differently in thought, word and deed in any particular circumstance.

And yet, with all our differences, we humans also have large-scale similarities. We all have the same primitive brain stem and any attempt to explain our behavior without including the effects of our primitive instincts is simply incomplete. Human nature is largely determined by those ancient instincts and is the primary "common denominator" of the similarities in human behavior. It is true that a few of our instincts are gender-specific and in males some are significantly enhanced by testosterone but, by and large, they are all basic human instincts.

As humans we are constantly required to make choices between what we want to do and what we feel we "should" do. The majority of our instincts are saying "me, me, me" but our laws, rules, conscience and religious teachings are saying "there are others to consider." Since everyone sees things from their own unique perspective, these conflicts cause different degrees of stress on different people. To the majority of us, most of these choices are fairly clear and not too difficult to make.

Most of us are essentially law-abiding and we often forego at least some of our interests in favor of what we "should" do. At the other end of the spectrum are those who have no trouble at all in making choices because they basically have no conscience at all. These people consider only their own wishes at the expense of all others. These are the criminals and predators who somehow failed to develop compassion and other humane qualities.

Somewhere between these two groups are the people with strong feelings of conscience and equally strong feelings for their own wants and desires. This creates a kind of an impasse that causes severe emotional stress much like sensory overload. Such unresolved conflicts can lead to the so-called "nervous breakdown" for those who must escape by dropping out rather that making a choice and living with it.

There is an old saying, "there is a little larceny in everyone." This is true but in some of us more so than others. We are all trying to do what we feel is best for ourselves and our loved ones within the moral, ethical and legal boundaries that we recognize. What is the difference between a "shrewd businessman" and a con artist? A surprising number of us are not only willing but even eager to "put one over" on others, especially strangers, for our personal gain.

Questionable tactics such as shoddy workmanship, use of poor quality materials, empty promises, false claims, and outright lies are just a few examples of behavior that requires a "buyer beware" attitude. Members of all species instinctively mistrust strangers because all strangers are potential enemies. Most humans have been taught to trust and often override this instinct but if we get burned too often, we tend to become very cautious and wary.

Noted economist, Adam Smith, saw the free marketplace in the early United States as self-regulating. He noted that if any individual or business took advantage of customers, competition would soon spring up and bring the cost of goods and services back to more reasonable levels. In general this is true but back in his day there were no mega-companies that could create monopolies and manipulate supplies of critical materials on a global scale.

Laws are an integral and necessary part of every society. Without laws there would be very little order primarily because of human nature. Most of us see the need for laws to apply to "all those other people" but we tend to feel that they really shouldn't apply to "me." From small things such as occasionally exceeding the speed limit to more serious crimes, most of us rationalize that there are times when we are justified in breaking certain laws and we gamble that we won't be caught.

In general, the majority of our species is committed to preserving human life. This is evident from things like the worldwide response to natural disasters such as tsunamis, hurricanes, earthquakes, famines etc. Caring people from many countries contribute time, effort, money and supplies to save as many lives as possible. This compassion is in stark contrast to the opposite side of human nature that can lead to willing and even eager participation in such horrendous atrocities such as "ethnic cleansing," the systematic murder of all men, women and children belonging to some particular religious, social or cultural group.

Even if there are other forms of intelligent life somewhere on other planets, we know for sure that there are no other humans anywhere. In the entire universe, we are unique and therefore it makes perfect sense that human life is precious and should be preserved. However, it also seems quite obvious that not all human life is precious. Hardened criminals who prey on the innocent basically have no regard for any life but their own. They have no redeeming virtues and after being convicted they should be executed or permanently institutionalized.

Far too many innocent people are maimed and murdered every year by repeat offenders who have already proven that they are not fit to be free in any society but are nevertheless pardoned, paroled or simply released. There is a popular adage that says, "capital punishment is not a deterrent to crime" which may or may not be true but there is one inescapable fact that cannot be argued. A murderer who has been executed will never kill again.

The extreme behavior of a person who commits horrible atrocities without remorse may actually be the result of a deranged mind. Mental impairment causes all sorts of bizarre behavior which may even be clinically diagnosed as "criminally insane" but the majority of people who commit these acts are not mentally impaired. They are simply people who choose not to override some of their basic human instincts.

We all have murderous thoughts especially when we are angry. We have all imagined and even wished that we could do horrible things to certain people in times of stress and rage. Of course, the majority of us decide against carrying out these dire thoughts.

When it comes to decisions that do not involve physically hurting someone, we all have our personal concepts of what is acceptable and what crosses our self-imposed lines. For most people the lines we draw for ourselves are somewhat less restrictive than those we feel are appropriate for others and, not surprisingly, some are quite flexible. They tend to shift depending on the size of potential reward, the odds of our being exposed and our perception of the possible retribution.

A basic part of our instinct of dominance is the drive to climb to a higher position. We may be members of any number of business, social, sports or intellectual hierarchies. Some of us feel we have already reached the level we've been striving for but most of us are still trying to advance. Our personal ethics and conscience greatly influence the tactics we use. The majority of us seem to always want more things, more money, more power and more control, in other words, more indicators of a higher status.

For example, do we really need luxury cars? What is the difference between a typical affordable car and a typical luxury car? Primarily it is the price and the name. There are ample moderately priced cars that offer the same amenities as the ridiculously expensive ones but they don't have the name. The same kind of thinking is true in relation to almost every facet of our lives. Humans, in general, favor conspicuous consumption. We want to advertise our success. We want to lord it over all those less affluent people. Why? Because it means that we have a higher position in some type of social hierarchy.

The more we can show off what we have and can afford, the higher we appear to rise on the social ladder. We like to feel that we occupy a high position because it means that we have more influence and control. People look up to us with respect, recognition and even admiration. We each want to be in the winners circle, to be one of the elite, to be on the A list, to be important.

This tendency is so common that it cannot be the result of individual decisions based on reason and logic. It has to be part of our instinctive "human nature." Two lines from a popular pop song of the 1980's say it as well as anyone can:

I was born to run ahead of the rest.
All I ever wanted was to be the best.

All over the United States and probably parts of other countries where incomes tend to be above average, hundreds of perfectly serviceable houses on large lots with 2000 to 5000 square feet of living space are being bought up just for the lots. The buyers are often newly affluent couples most of whom do not even have children living with them. These people pay full market price for the houses and then simply tear them down and replace them with palatial estates of 10,000 to 30,000 square feet of space.

The most common verbal justification for this is that they are finally getting their "dream home" and they decorate it lavishly inside and out. Some remain satisfied for years but if their income doubles or triples, many of the "dream homes" start to look drab. Incredibly, the owners may even feel they need more room.

Logically, no two people need that much space and all those expensive trappings so the real reason is the conspicuous show of status symbols that are meant to tell the world, "We have made it." Rich people have traditionally lived overtly lavish and even decadent life styles and that seems to be the standard that the rest of us admire and are striving to attain.

There is an old adage that says, in so many words; "Human needs are quite modest but human wants are unlimited." The drive to accumulate more showy symbols of success and climb to ever-higher positions in the hierarchy of our societies is simply a manifestation of our ancient instinct of dominance. Applying some logic and reason to this instinctive drive could go a long way toward preventing much of the tremendous waste of our precious natural resources as well as the misery and premature death that can be directly attributed to this ancient calling.

People in all social strata feel various emotions such as contempt, indifference or pity for those who are less affluent. There are several reasons why some people do not have as much as we do. They may be less ambitious, less educated, not as well qualified, not as intelligent or simply not as lucky. As humans, we can't help but feel a certain pride and smugness as we look down on them. Whether we show it or not most of us like this feeling. The higher we climb and the more wealth we have, the more people we can look down on.

Pride in ourselves and what we have accomplished gives us a good feeling and is a positive emotion. Taking pride in showy displays of opulence and conspicuous consumption meant to advertise our social position is simply obeying an ancient, outdated instinct without questioning its validity.

In progressive societies that allow personal freedoms, the opportunities for individual expression are virtually unlimited. For the most part, we humans do not want to be anonymous. We want to be noticed, to be seen as individuals, not just another face in the crowd. We instinctively want to belong to groups of like-minded people. Smaller groups are more likely to be like-minded and cohesive than larger ones.

There is a well-known saying, "It is better to be a big fish in a small pond than . . . ." Since we can't all be big fish, most of us feel that a fish of any size is more likely to find recognition in a smaller pond. The saying does not literally mean small town versus big city because it refers to the size of the peer group rather than the surrounding area.

Our penchant for identifying with groups explains why so many of them exist and the awesome versatility of our large brains explains why the groups are so varied. In all facets of our lives, from hobbies to social circles to religion, we seek out others with similar ideas, beliefs, attitudes and ways of acting, thinking and speaking. We want to be among friends who look forward to seeing us. We enjoy being the center of attention and being important in some manner. It is normally quite satisfying and pleasurable to be in a place "where everybody knows your name."

We may not all want to be group leaders but we do want to be in a position that causes our peers to look up to us to some degree and show us a measure of recognition, respect and appreciation. We want to be "somebody." The majority of us are able to satisfy these wishes by cultivating some "specialty" that sets us apart from the crowd, something we can be proud of, something we feel is unique.

Most of us have at least one "specialty" that brings us attention and positive feedback. It may be a musical talent, an aptitude or interest in one or more sports, a knack for something, a collection of some sort, a great recipe, a job skill, a hobby or any number of others. Whatever our "claim to fame" may be, we take serious pride in it. Most specialties are considered to be normal and common but in growing societies, less common activities become more numerous.

Some of the more unusual interests may be seen by the general public as frivolous, far out or even ridiculous but they actually serve an important function by providing additional avenues for more people to express their uniqueness and originality. Such activities as fashion shows for pets, beauty pageants for little girls, modern art that seems to make no sense, little known sports such as Irish Road Bowling, keeping exotic pets, hot dog eating contests and a myriad of others may be scoffed at by the majority of us but they mean a great deal to the participants.

As long as these endeavors cause no harm to anyone, they should be viewed as beneficial and positive. Most of us are satisfied with recognition from our peers while others strive for wider exposure; at least our "fifteen minutes of fame" and some of us won't rest till we achieve fame or notoriety.

It is normally very important for young people, especially teens, to be seen as separate and different from the "old fogies" of the previous generation while still maintaining a peer group identity. Body piercing, unusual hairstyles, outlandish clothing, playing loud, controversial music and inventing new slang words and symbols that are unique to the group members are just a few of the tactics used by younger generations to show that they are part of the "modern world" rather than the outdated past.

Often, young people who have not yet found a positive specialty to claim as their own resort to negative activities. Generally, the feeling is that even negative attention is better than no attention at all. It is normal for young people to rebel in some manner against authority as they are trying to assert their independence. They are simply practicing to become independent adults.

Much of this rebelliousness, while annoying to adults, is basically harmless but decisions about drugs, alcohol, fast cars, weapons, sexually transmitted diseases, gangs and dozens of other options must be made by individuals with limited life experience.

Young people with a strong need for attention who have no specialty that can get them praise and positive feedback often engage in bizarre behavior just to be noticed. Many become frustrated adults with no hope of achieving the prominence and respect they crave. Some of these unhappy people resort to extreme measures.

One good example is Lynette "Squeaky" Fromme who made an unsuccessful but very public attempt to assassinate President Gerald Ford in 1972. Why? She had no credible explanation. Also why did John Hinckley shoot President Ronald Reagan with full media coverage? Why did Mark David Chapman kill pop idol John Lennon in full view of fans and papparazi?

These three young people had no political or social agenda. They had no great cause for which to sacrifice their lives and freedom. In fact, they had no real interest in any specific area. Their motive cannot be explained as simple domination over other human beings or they would have targeted some ordinary citizens or children and carried it out in secret. People who kill for their own pleasure prey on unknowns, not presidents and celebrities surrounded by television crews.

Whether or not they will ever admit it, the most reasonable explanation is that they just could no longer stand to be anonymous. It was time for the world to know their names, to acknowledge that they were somebody, not just faceless unknowns. They had to be seen as individuals, as people of substance with some type of "claim to fame," even if only notoriety.

Sometimes even serial killers can't stand to be anonymous forever. Dennis Rader of Wichita, Kansas, also known as BTK which stands for Bind, Torture and Kill, got away with murder for thirty years and would never have been caught except for his own need to be seen as someone of importance. At first, the ultimate domination over his victims was enough to satisfy him but soon he felt the need for recognition for his skill in evading capture. He sent letters to the local newspaper taunting the authorities.

Eventually, even national media coverage was not enough because it was his alter ego, the faceless BTK, who was getting the credit, not Dennis Rader. He finally sent out enough clues to lead the police to him. He readily confessed to ten murders and calmly described them in detail to the interrogators with whom he felt a kinship because he said he had also been in "law enforcement." He was referring to the fact that he had served as a uniformed Animal Control Officer for the city of Wichita. In interviews it was quite apparent that he felt he was finally getting the recognition he so richly deserved. Prison and death row were obviously preferable to remaining anonymous.

Members of most mammal species have a built-in bias against those who do not appear to be "normal." Mothers in all species nourish and protect their young even those born with handicaps but other group members are normally not as accepting. There are documented cases of adult chimpanzees killing young chimps with deformities after the youngsters got old enough to stray away from their mothers. Except for the maternal instinct, which is common to all females, chimp society has no "right to life" concept.

What was your first thought the last time you were approached by a stranger with a physical disability who also appeared to be mentally impaired? Initially you probably wanted to turn around and go the other way. If you made eye contact, you may have forced a smile, perhaps mumbled "Hi" and kept moving. We humans have that same built-in bias concerning disabilities and people who are "different."

If we are alone our first instinct is to avoid the handicapped, especially if they appear at all erratic. Sadly, humans in groups who feel the safety of numbers can easily slip into the "lynch mob mentality" and be quite cruel to the mentally and physically impaired.

We are verbally, physically and/or psychologically abusive to others only when we are quite sure there will be no retribution. We may wish to do all manner of terrible things to various people but we do not act on these feelings if we fear the consequences. Those who bully, mock, embarrass, make fun of, or abase others in any way do not feel threatened, at least not at the time. They see themselves in a dominant position and expect the victim to be submissive, which is quite often what happens.

If the victim produces a weapon or a big mean-looking bodyguard shows up, everything changes and the would-be dominator quickly becomes submissive. We have all seen this behavior in both adults and children. Young children who have not learned to suppress their instinctive feelings are normally quite cruel to other children who are "different." Those who stutter or lisp are mocked. Those with visible birth defects, large burns or scars, flyaway ears, crossed eyes or excess weight are stared at, laughed at and ridiculed. Those afflicted with Autism, Downs Syndrome, tics and spasms or simply below average IQ are often insulted, shunned and scorned.

Even those who are simply too poor to afford the latest styles of "in" clothing may be ostracized and snubbed. Thoughtless and mean-spirited treatment such as this can be devastating to children who already feel that they have some defect and are trying desperately to fit in.

Since we value human life and try to keep everyone alive regardless of physical or mental condition, a significant number of children fall into these categories. People of all ages with these "abnormalities" suffer varying degrees of pain and discomfort from the condition itself but the negative reactions they see and hear from their fellow humans may be the worst pain of all. Lack of acceptance by one's peers has been known to cause severe emotional distress which can contribute to depression, substance abuse, "nervous breakdowns" and even suicide.

Formal courses explaining inherent human behaviors and how to handle them should begin in kindergarten and continue through all levels of education. The aim of these courses should be to provide young people with an understanding of "human nature" and the knowledge that acting on some of our very normal and natural feelings can be quite hurtful to others.

As yet no formal courses exist but some dedicated, independent thinking teachers have created role-playing scenarios in which all their students have the opportunity to be the victims as well as the oppressors. They all get to feel first-hand both sides of prejudice and psychological abuse. The scenarios are then discussed at length by the class as a group. The teacher encourages each student to share the feelings of anger, fear, injustice, inferiority, smugness, arrogance, superiority or power that they experienced.

This type of training seems to be an invaluable first step for all young people and should be expanded to include a thorough explanation of why dominant behavior is so common in humans as well as other species. The primary point should be that as humans, we can and should choose to be kind, tolerant and supportive to others rather than unkind, intolerant and cruel. Even if our initial reaction to a person or a situation is negative, we can stop and think for a moment and make a decision based on reason rather than emotion.

Probably since the beginning of our species, another inherent behavior pattern and automatic response to others has been that external appearance is a prime consideration for the majority of us. One of Mark Twain's notable sayings is, "Clothes make the man. Naked people have very little influence in society." As humorous as this is, the basic premise is true. Clothes are extremely important to us. We humans have used a wide variety of clothing as well as accessories, makeup and body art, not only to enhance our appearance but also to indicate our positions in society. Long before civilization was invented, clothing progressed from being strictly functional, e.g. warmth, protection and modesty, to being decorative, image enhancing and position defining. Even before we graduated from animal skins to cloth, we created variations which were intended more for appearance than utility.

Non-functional headgear was probably one of the very early forms of adornment as well as an indicator of status and position, a practice that is still very much in use today. Some examples are crowns, tiaras, stovepipe hats, judicial wigs, most uniform hats and caps, large religious headpieces and a myriad of others. They serve no practical purpose but are nonetheless considered indispensable to those who wear them. With certain exceptions such as surgical caps, hard hats and the like, essentially all headgear worn indoors is worn for effect rather than utility.

Clothing and other adornments have become so important to most of us because they are the primary instruments we use to "make a statement" about who we are. What are we trying to say? The statement is meant to make it plain to all who see us that we are unique individuals and we occupy a specific position in society.

We often go to great lengths to portray the image of how we wish to be seen even if we suspect it is not entirely genuine. Many of us spend more than we can reasonably afford to appear more affluent, more successful, more influential and more attractive than we actually are or feel we are.

Jewelry is considered to be one of the most important adornments in most societies. Early jewelry probably consisted of necklaces of animal teeth and bones that signified hunting prowess or perhaps clan affiliation with a certain animal species. As soon as the technology became available, precious stones such as diamonds and rubies and rare metals such as gold and silver became the standard raw materials for fine jewelry.

The beauty and relative scarcity of the gems and ores plus the time and skill required to make them into beautiful baubles made them very expensive and as such they became indicators of wealth and power. Elaborate crowns, necklaces, medallions, rings and chests of gold and gems became the hallmarks of royalty.

Wealthy people accumulated jewelry and used it in ostentatious displays of affluence. This tradition has continued into modern times even though beautiful imitations can now be mass-produced quite cheaply. Gems such as diamonds are no longer in short supply but they retain their high value because they are in demand by so many people. They are considered to be secure investments and have been used to buy everything from food to freedom in times of war and runaway inflation when money becomes virtually worthless.

Even though only trained jewelers can distinguish between real and fake diamonds, the real ones are still considered mandatory by virtually everyone as indicators of opulence and wealth. To prevent theft, many people keep their real jewelry hidden away in safes and have cheap, exact replicas made to wear and/or put on display. Since the copies are indistinguishable from the real thing, this suggests that the primary purpose of the real gems is as an indicator of prestige rather than a means of adornment.

Because they are so hard, diamonds have some important industrial applications such as cutting tools and drills but those uses in no way justify the value placed on them. As long as we humans continue to demand them for jewelry, they will be expensive but logic and reason suggest that, like so many other adornments in our societies, they are highly overrated.

In retrospect, it is apparent why gems and gold initially became so highly prized but it is hard to see why they remain so today. We could just as easily attach our aspirations and sentimental values to equally beautiful but much more affordable jewelry.

This inborn tendency to think of our own wants and needs in the short term is causing some serious long-term consequences for our planet and all it's inhabitants. Like most other species, we humans have a tremendous potential for reproduction but unrestrained reproduction in any species has disastrous results.

Every species that has ever existed has experienced "boom and bust" population fluctuations. When times are favorable a species can flourish and multiply rapidly. During harsh conditions such as prolonged drought or other natural phenomena, massive numbers of individuals die of thirst, starvation and disease. Long-term climate changes have led to the extinction of literally millions of species.

Since the beginning of the human species, our population has been increasing, slowly at first but the growth accelerated exponentially after civilization became established. Because of our large brains we have been able to create more "boom" conditions than "busts" but, logically, we cannot keep reproducing at our present, ever-increasing rate.

Technology has vastly improved our ability to produce food but technology has limits and at some point in the not-too-distant future we will undoubtedly exceed the capacity of our planet to support our numbers. Unless we take some action soon, there will eventually be famine on a global scale such as we have never seen.

Logically, this says that we must take realistic steps to slow down population growth all over the world. More premature deaths from war, disease, famine etc is not a realistic step. Neither is expecting people to refrain from having sex. Education in conjunction with effective birth control is the most realistic and potentially attainable solution. Statistics show that birth rates per capita are significantly lower in developed countries where birth control methods, family planning and good medical care are available.

Millions of people reject birth control for religious reasons and billions more reject it because the odds that existing children will survive to become adults are quite poor. Population experts generally agree that most people would soon limit their personal reproduction if the survival rate of their children could be dramatically improved and if simple, cheap birth control methods were made available.

In most cultures, having a lot of children is considered a normal, natural and positive thing to do. Without a doubt, large families provide a wonderful source of love, comfort, support, warmth, pride, satisfaction and security for billions of humans. Numerous books, plays, TV shows and movies extol the joys, interactions and just plain fun of having a lot of siblings and/or a houseful of kids.

Unfortunately, large families are becoming a liability for our species rather than an asset. History provides us with many examples, in all species including humans, which show that overpopulation inevitably leads to high rates of premature death. The world's food production is currently more than adequate to feed all the people on earth but even a small climate change could easily reduce that to less than adequate. And what happens in a few decades if the current trend continues and the population has doubled?

Probably the best example of what our planet is facing is already happening on a smaller scale in China. For at least the last two decades, China has had laws in place that severely restrict family size. The Chinese lawmakers did not arrive at this radical decision lightly. They were not just being petty, arbitrary or mean-spirited. Literally millions of people had to die of starvation before the government faced the harsh reality that their country simply could not support the existing population, much less the projected increase.

Despite the tremendous effort to incorporate modern industrialization and production methods, the Chinese population would soon outrun the country's ability to provide enough food if birth rates were unchecked. Even with the current family size restrictions, their numbers are increasing and a catastrophe such as a prolonged drought would lead to significant starvation.

For any country or area of the world, up to and including the entire planet, there is an optimum population level and a maximum sustainable level. The optimum level is small enough to comfortably feed and house the inhabitants without causing permanent damage to the environment. At this level, the self-regulating mechanisms of the planet allow it to recover from any scars or mistreatment caused by human activity. Since the beginning of civilization, various localized areas have experienced temporary overpopulation but for the planet as a whole, human numbers have been at or below the optimum level for at least 99.9% of the time our species has existed. Most experts agree that we have already exceeded this optimum level.

There are disturbing indications that we may be asking for more than our planet can safely provide. Thousands of acres of productive land have already been depleted and ruined by overfarming and overgrazing. Thousands more have been covered over by cities, developments and roads. Vast areas of tropical rain forests and other forests have been cleared by loggers and farmers, significantly reducing the earth's potential to absorb excess carbon dioxide. Pollution in the atmosphere, oceans and rivers indicate over production of goods, overuse of resources and excessive use of fossil fuel energy. Altogether, these indicators suggest that we are fast approaching the maximum sustainable population level and there appears to be no hint of a slowdown.

People who limit the size of their families tend to do so because of health or other personal reasons but very few voluntarily limit reproduction specifically for population control. There are some dedicated people trying to spread the word but without much success. Even dire predictions of future events are no match for the combined influences of human sex drive, maternal and paternal instinct, culture, custom and religious teachings.

Another factor that must be considered here is the profit motive. Unregulated Capitalism as practiced by most of the world today relies on ever-increasing markets for more and more products. Zero or very low population growth would severely diminish the demand for goods and services.

The solution to this dilemma is quite easy to see but will be very difficult to achieve, at least in the near future. First, all humans must be made aware of what we are facing. Then we must all choose reason over instinct and emotion. Easier said than done!

Most people know very little about population dynamics but the inescapable fact is that every population "boom" in every species that has ever existed has resulted in a "bust." In every "bust" a significant percentage of the population dies prematurely. A primary contributor to every "boom" has been an extended period of favorable climate and, directly or indirectly, the primary killer has been climate change.

The uncontrolled population increase that we are currently experiencing cannot continue indefinitely. There will be a "bust," we just don't know how soon it will happen or what will trigger it. We can minimize the loss of life and property with sensible planning and preparing or we can rush headlong over the cliff like lemmings.

The solution requires the vast majority of us to exercise restraint in our reproduction as well as most other areas of our lives and to practice tolerance and cooperation. To be prepared, we must put our time, effort and money into research and development of sensible technology that will prevent or at least lessen the impact of future disasters.

We are certainly capable of doing all this but will we actually do it? And, if so, will we begin in time to be effective?

So far, China is the only large country to enact laws restricting reproduction but in the near future, birth rates world-wide must be reduced either voluntarily or involuntarily. The consequences for our grandchildren and their children of uncontrolled population growth are too gruesome to contemplate. This is just one of the possible calamities of the future but it is one that we can plainly see coming. We cannot afford to ignore it and leave it for the next generation to deal with. We must start soon with at least some initial positive steps to limit our runaway population before massive numbers of people start paying the ultimate price.

Realistic population data and projections will eventually influence changes in cultural and religious doctrine for the benefit of humans everywhere. We humans have the brains and bodies that have enabled us to seriously modify our entire planet. We have the ability to make decisions based on logic and the comprehension to foresee possible consequences of those decisions. We also have the free will to overcome any of our primitive instincts that are no longer appropriate.

We have been granted stewardship of our world and all it's inhabitants and we simply cannot say, "No matter how dire our future may appear, God will take care of us." God gave us the ability and the responsibility to take care of our planet and everything on it.

Currently only a small percentage of our population is genuinely concerned about our long-term future but clearly the problems are global in nature and can only be solved by global solutions. The solutions can only succeed if the majority of individuals in the world are aware of the problems and are willing to participate in a collective effort to make the necessary changes.

To be effective these changes will require some hard decisions and some sacrifices that may seem initially painful. We will have to make some major revisions to our current way of thinking concerning status, wealth and material possessions.

This may seem like a monumental task but simply being aware that we do have outdated, primitive instincts should make a major difference in our willingness to disregard them and base our decisions on facts and reason rather than emotion and personal gain.

Most of us have only a rudimentary knowledge of volcanoes. The most recent example here in the United States was Mount Saint Helens in 1980. It was certainly a significant eruption but compared to others in the deeper past, it was relatively minor. The human death toll was less than 70, property loss was estimated at about three billion dollars and there was no measurable effect on the climate.

In 1815, a volcano called Tambora on a Malaysian island erupted with a force many times greater than that of Mt. St. Helens. Since it was an island, loss of life and property was not large but millions of tons of dust and ash were blown into the upper atmosphere and the climate of the entire Northern Hemisphere was affected.

The winter started early that year and was harsher than usual but the worst part was yet to come. When spring came it was still too cold for green plants to bloom and grow. Both wild and domestic animals had very little to graze on and the cold continued. 1816 became known as "the year without a summer." Most grains and other above ground crops would not grow. It snowed even in July and August. Many people had emergency stores of food but by autumn, the poorer people were trying to subsist on insects, rats and weeds. Over the following winter, millions of people died of starvation or diseases that most could have easily survived with better nutrition. By spring, enough ash and dust had settled out of the air so that the weather was nearly back to normal but it took several more years for the shattered economies to recover completely.

What would happen if there were another eruption and we had another year without a summer? The developed countries have a lot more stored food now but there are also a lot more people to feed. If 70% to 80% of the above ground crops in the Northern Hemisphere failed even for one year, how many people would starve? And what if it lasted longer that one year? Would everyone get a share of the existing food supplies? Without a massive attitude change, the "haves" would hoard and the "have-nots" would die. Not a pleasant thought! It doesn't have to be this way but unless we start seriously thinking and planning ahead, a scenario such as this, or worse, is inevitable.

There is convincing scientific evidence that our planet is entering a period of global warming. Science has determined that the earth has a history of climate changes most of which occur gradually. The data shows temperature extremes ranging from the entire world covered with ice to an overheated planet with no ice at all. Most of the variations have been significantly less than those two extremes and alternate between ice ages and very warm periods that may last from a few hundred years to a few hundred thousand years. Between the highs and lows are long stretches of moderate climate.

Our earth has been experiencing an extended period of moderate climate since the last ice age ended but during the last few hundred years the average global temperature has begun to increase. All indications are that this is part of a normal fluctuation and that the warming will continue. There is also scientific proof that human activity is significantly accelerating this trend. Especially since the Industrial Revolution we have been injecting pollutants and excess carbon dioxide into the atmosphere increasing the "greenhouse effect" which slows the normal loss of heat from the surface of the earth.

Governments all over the world are reluctant to impose restrictions on carbon dioxide emissions because of the negative effect they would have on industry. Short-term profits and cheap energy sources seem more important than long-term safety for future generations.

Former Vice-president, Al Gore, is one of the few politicians who is genuinely concerned and actively trying to educate as many people as possible on the seriousness of global warming. For years he traveled the United States and other countries with a slide show showing documented ecological calamities happening all over the world. This compelling presentation contained such facts as before and after pictures of glaciers that have existed for centuries and have all but disappeared in the last few decades. It emphasized significant meteorological and environmental changes that have already occurred and warned of more to come.

In 2006 Mr. Gore compiled his considerable research, expertise and experience into a beautifully illustrated book entitled "An Inconvenient Truth." This excellent book contains crucial information that all humans need to be aware of. He also produced a critically acclaimed documentary film based on the book.

The June 25, 2006 issue of the Parade magazine featured an excellent article by Eugene Linden entitled "Why You Can't Ignore the Changing Climate." The article emphasizes the significant increase in loss of life and destruction of property from natural causes in recent decades that is directly attributed to global warming. It also points out that the resultant financial burdens from these catastrophes are not limited to those in the directly affected areas. Higher insurance premiums, taxes, prices for goods and services, energy costs, etc are affecting us all and there is no letup in sight.

Mr. Linden's most recent book, "The Winds of Change; Climate, Weather and the Destruction of Civilizations," documents the profound effects of climate changes on past civilizations. We cannot afford to go on with business as usual and let history repeat itself.

As the average global temperature continues to climb, more media attention is being focused on the effects and consequences. Increasingly, well-known people from many walks of life are offering their names and services to the task of disseminating this crucial knowledge. This is definitely a reason for optimism because until the majority of us are aware of what is happening and what must be done about it, efforts to change may be too little and too late.

In July, 2006 several cable TV channels including the Science channel and the Discovery channel began airing a two-hour special called "Global Warming, What You Should Know." This excellent presentation is skillfully hosted and narrated by former NBC newscaster, Tom Brokaw and contains excerpts from interviews with some of the world's foremost authorities on the causes and effects of global weather variations. Awareness of this critical information offers an opportunity for all of us to participate in the prevention of a global catastrophe.

The first step in slowing down this excessive warming trend is to apply some reason and moderation to our excessive demands for energy and non-essential products. At the same time we must start decreasing the amount of money and resources expended on destructive and frivolous pursuits and put more into developing technology to deal with all types of disasters.

It is well documented that the polar ice caps are melting at an alarming rate releasing huge quantities of fresh water into the oceans. The oceans have large-scale currents, such as the Gulf Stream and the Alaskan Current, that act like giant conveyer belts carrying warm water to the polar regions and cold water to the tropics. The resulting heat transfer moderates the climate all over the globe. It has been reliably established that excessive fresh water from melting ice caps can shut down these salt-water conveyer belts. That would initiate the rapid onset of another ice age. We don't know when this will happen but we do know that it is inevitable at some point if global warming continues.

Every climate change takes a heavy toll on species that have adapted completely to very specific environments. If these species cannot readapt to the changing conditions, they become extinct. Climate changes have caused literally millions of extinctions. Creatures with varied diets that can cope with a wide range of temperatures have the best chance of survival. There are currently many species of plants and animals that are on the verge of extinction and some of these will be gone during this century if our average temperature continues to climb. Many thousands more will perish during the next ice age.

Global warming is just one of the big challenges we must soon deal with for the sake of our grandchildren and their descendants. We can use our ever-expanding technology to survive and prosper if we plan ahead. In the short term, we need to conserve resources and drastically cut harmful emissions and pollutants. In the long term, our positive steps must include conserving resources and increasing food production.

These necessary changes plus several others which are equally important, can all be achieved if we direct our technology toward positive ends rather than destructive or frivolous pursuits such as making war, controlling others and conspicuous consumption. It is simply a matter of the majority of humans making positive choices such as tolerance, cooperation and moderation instead of our more destructive primitive instincts.

CHAPTER 10

Our Future

Humans have a tremendous capacity for positive virtues such as kindness, caring, tolerance, cooperation and love plus a long, rich history of stunning achievements, amazing technological advancements, magnificent art, music and literature. We also have a horrendous legacy of hatred, war, conquest, murder, torture, slavery and destruction. Do we really need both extremes? Can we keep the positives without the negatives? Can we exist and prosper with only peaceful, non-violent competition?

These are serious questions because, as of the present time, we have not made much progress toward eliminating or even decreasing the negatives. Evolutionary changes take hundreds of thousands of years so we cannot expect any changes to our primitive brain stems in the foreseeable future. The fate of our species rests with the decision-making ability of the larger sections of our brains.

History is full of examples of evil despots who were and still are hated by almost everyone who knew of them because they were responsible for so much pain, suffering and death. But what about the "good guys?" History books extol the virtues of rulers such as "Alexander the Great" of ancient Macedonia. What was so great about him?

Like many other well-known rulers, Alexander was "great" because he was a military genius. Almost from birth he was trained to be a warrior. While still in his teens he became the leader of his country's cavalry and by his early twenties he was the ruler. He did a lot more than simply defend his country. By the time he died at about age 30, he had defeated the mighty Persian Empire and conquered most of the known world.

Alexander was a perfect example of the classic alpha male so prominent in all species. A superb physical specimen, he trained his soldiers, gave them the best weapons and led them into every battle. To a man they followed him with unquestioning loyalty. With his brilliant tactics and the skill and devotion of his men, he never lost a battle. He defeated forces up to ten times the size of his army. In some battles, he would lose up to a thousand men but the other side normally lost at least ten times more.

In Alexander's short career he was undoubtedly responsible for the deaths of several million people and the enslavement of countless others as well as massive destruction, looting, pillaging and rape. But by our standards, he was a "great" man because he had achieved the ultimate; for a time, he was the alpha male of the world. He "united" the known world into one large empire. The fact that none of the countries wanted to be "united" was irrelevant.

What did Alexander do that was different from any other dictator aspiring to rule a large part of the world? The primary difference was that he was always a winner, right up the time of his death. Most dictators, such as Hitler, are initially successful but eventually defeated. If Hitler had conquered Russia and then the United States, would he go down in history as "Adolph the Great"?

This brings up some more very important questions. Do we need winners like Alexander to admire and losers like Hitler to hate? Does the majority of our species require this kind of aggression, conquering, dominance and struggle to make life worthwhile? Can we lead satisfying, rewarding lives without the warfare, self-sacrifice, bravery and glory? Can we get enough of the emotional highs that come with victory, triumph and conquest from more Olympic games and less armed conflict? Can we be satisfied with making war on hunger, poverty, disease, natural disasters and criminals rather than other societies?

Many people live modest, contented lives doing good deeds, helping others, setting examples of peace, tolerance and love. These are the real heroes who deserve our respect and admiration but only a few such as Gandhi and Mother Teresa have gotten any real recognition. There are some concerned people who are trying to change this trend and bring more public attention to individuals engaged in humanitarian efforts.

In June and July of 2005, a series called "The New Heroes" was aired on PBS television. It was backed, hosted and narrated by Robert Redford and it showcased compassionate entrepreneurs who have created jobs, income and hope for thousands of disadvantaged people in some of the poorest areas of the world. These men and women will never be "rich and famous" and their businesses will never be represented on a stock exchange but they have literally saved thousands of people from starvation and countless more from lives of hopeless poverty. None of these efforts were meant to be charity. They were meant to provide something much more important than charity; opportunity.

Is it possible for humans, with our instinctive propensity for violence, to shift our attention from action heroes, military conquerors and alpha males to the Gandhis and the Mother Teresas of the world? Can we actually idolize those who dedicate themselves to fighting hopelessness and despair rather than fighting other nations?

Large numbers of people in every society of the world have chosen to suppress their destructive instincts and live quiet, peaceful, non-violent lives except possibly in the case of self-defense. It seems that if some of us can do it, the rest of us should be able to also, but that may not be true.

Is it realistic to think that most humans can find fulfillment in peaceful competition? It's all a matter of individual choice but what could possibly convince the majority of individual humans to override their most destructive instincts? As a start, awareness of the very existence of primitive instincts in humans seems crucial.

For a species to prosper in the "survival of the fittest" mode, essentially all instincts must be geared toward putting one's own needs and safety first. It can be described as "looking out for number one." In fact, completely unrestrained instinctive behavior would have to be described as "extremely selfish."

Other than the submission part of dominance and submission, there is only one altruistic instinct that will override this obsession with one's own welfare and that is the protection of one's group. Adult members of all species will give their lives in defense of their group. Whether defending their own territory or invading another group's territory, individuals willingly fight to the death. We humans do the same to protect our loved ones, families, friends, religion and nation; our group.

The teen years are especially hard for most people. It is a sort of a limbo between childhood and adult status and most teens want the advantages of being an adult along with the limited responsibilities of being a child. They see the endless variety of luxuries and entertainment that are available to those with money. Raging hormones tend to magnify teen emotions and elevate their wants almost to the point of being obsessions and many get very angry at the injustice they feel. "Those other people have so much and I have so little. It's not fair. I should have everything I want and nobody should be able to tell me what to do."

There is nothing unusual about these thoughts. They are quite normal. If there are opportunities for education and jobs, eventually most teens get a pretty clear picture of the world and turn into responsible adults. Others never adjust and turn to gangs, crime, violence and suicide.

Some individuals survive their teen years only to become angry adults with numerous grudges and diminished tolerance for rules and authority. These are the people who never learned to suppress their selfish instincts in favor of more selfless behavior such as kindness, cooperation and tolerance. Some of these people are like time bombs ready to explode.

Nearly every day we hear about one or more murders. If the perpetrators are adults in their thirties or older and they are first time offenders, we may ask "What in the world caused that person to do such a thing?" We may assume the killer was just an average person somehow driven over the edge. Chances are that person was never a well-adjusted, tolerant individual and the unresolved anger and pent-up feelings of frustration, self-pity and injustice finally came to a peak. One of those time bombs that finally reached the zero time.

We all experience intense negative emotions from time to time but normal, well-adjusted humans are able to work through them and, over time, dump them like so much garbage. Those who choose to keep these hateful thoughts alive and uppermost in their minds can be compared to an atomic pile that slowly gets hotter and hotter until, at some point, it reaches critical mass. The sad part is that, except for people who mentally impaired, it's all a matter of personal choice.

High schools and even elementary schools all over the United States and the rest of the world contain many little dominance hierarchies that reflect all the negative aspects of adult society. All forms of physical and mental control such as humiliation, bullying, coercion, theft, protection rackets, and sexual harassment are common. The groups may have labels such as "the clique", "the in crowd" or "the snobs" or they may have specific gang names. Physical aggression is more apparent with the male groups and psychological cruelty is more common with the females.

These groups are not simply young people imitating what they see grown-ups doing. They are acting out instinctive behavior that feels completely natural to them without thinking about the effect it has on the victims. Everyone has the same instinct to dominate whomever they can and submit to whomever they have to, but of course, millions of people of all ages suppress these instincts in favor of more rational behavior.

Anyone who has raised or studied small children has seen unrestrained instinctive behavior. Initially, the only concept babies have is their own wants and needs. As they get a little older and are required to share, their first reaction is "No way, that's mine." Selfishness is completely natural. Children learn to share because they have to, not because they want to.

Children instinctively submit to their parent's wishes because they must but some do it more willingly than others. Most learn the benefits of cooperation and sharing from interaction with other children as well as parental guidance. Those who learn these lessons early are usually the happiest and most well-adjusted. There is an old expression; "Happiness is getting your way" but how many truly spoiled children have you seen that are actually happy?

If children were taught, both at home and at school starting no later than kindergarten, why humans have these reactions, they would grow up knowing that all instinctive feelings are normal and natural but that doesn't mean they are all acceptable. It should be continually reinforced that only animals have no choice in how they behave, but humans can decide which feelings to act on and which to ignore. Suppressing negative and destructive tendencies would gradually become a normal way of life for children raised with this knowledge.

The old excuses such as "the devil made me do it" or "I can't help it, there's a demon inside me" are no longer believable. Modern science has proven that our "dark side" does not come from devils or demons. "Human nature" has its primary roots in our primitive brain stem and only the other uniquely human parts of our brain can control how we deal with it. Evil voices, regardless of their origin, cannot force us to do anything. Each individual is totally responsible for his or her own actions.

It would be naïve to suggest that this type of training would guarantee that all children would grow into peace-loving, tolerant adults. Even when the whole world finally has access to quality, science-based education, there will probably always be a significant number of "bad guys" among us. They are the evil people who will follow their worst instincts regardless of what they know or how they have been trained. Dealing with these predators will continue to be a massive challenge for the "good guys."

Like all other species, we humans are hard-wired for adversity. Since the beginning of life on earth, all organisms have had to struggle against all manner of adversity just so some could survive. Civilization has finally made it possible to accumulate the knowledge, skill and technology that allows large numbers of us to live peaceful, tranquil lives.

Not surprisingly, most of us are not completely adjusted to peace and security. Most of us actually feel more natural when we have some adversity. If we have no big troubles or worries, we tend to make mountains out of molehills. We have all been guilty of getting all stirred up about some very insignificant issues when our lives are otherwise progressing smoothly.

There are many real problems that we should be focusing our energy on instead of trivial stuff. Earthquakes, tsunamis, hurricanes, floods, droughts, pandemic diseases, the dwindling ozone layer etc. are all legitimate, ongoing concerns that need major attention and effort to minimize loss of life and property.

Less evident but even more important for future generations are the mega-disasters which have occurred regularly in the past and are sure to happen again but we just don't know when. Science has determined that the earth has periodically been subjected to ice ages. The last one ended about 10,000 years ago. There will be another at some future time. Will we be ready? Giant volcanoes in conjunction with mega-earthquakes have laid waste to entire countries. They are normal and natural results of global plate tectonics, the movement of earth's landmasses. We need to devote serious effort and resources to determine where the next ones may be and get ready for them. Gigantic meteors and asteroids have struck the earth and caused unimaginable devastation. These and other horrendous disasters have occurred periodically in our planet's violent past causing massive destruction and untold loss of life forms.

These are all serious concerns that we should be planning and preparing for but the majority of humans aren't even aware of them and many who are aware are more concerned about personal details that seem much more pressing. From petty squabbles to all out war, most of us are more concerned about day to day living than potential disasters that may or may not happen during our lifetimes. Nevertheless, one or more of these disasters will very likely happen before this century is over and could easily contribute to the end of a significant portion of the larger living species on earth, including humans.

We have the intelligence and technology to minimize the effects of any disaster if we can cooperate and work together for the benefit of all life on earth.

We humans are, by nature, opposed to change and most older adults in the world today will not make any major change in their actions or their way of thinking during the remainder of their lives. But just think of what a few generations of young people could accomplish if they were aware of the origin of our more destructive "animal instincts" and decided not to follow them. It would be the start of a new direction for our species, one that millions of peaceful humans have dreamed of and yearned for since the beginning of civilization.

At some point in the future, there would be no more need for war so all the time, effort and money that goes into military forces, military equipment and reconstruction in the aftermath of war could be put into peaceful pursuits.

There could be a massive, concentrated effort to minimize loss of life and property due to natural disasters. The population explosion could be slowed and eventually stopped with world-wide family planning and effective birth control rather than infant mortality and other premature deaths.

With a little rethinking about what is important, we could stop ravaging and polluting our environment for profit and insure that everyone has access to sanitary water and food. Our aggressive tendencies could be channeled into police work; capturing, rehabilitating, incarcerating or eliminating the criminals and evil degenerates who prey on innocent victims.

This radical change would take a world-wide effort but it must start with individual people. The majority of humans, regardless of status, position, race, religion, nationality and culture must make the commitment to suppress their normal destructive instincts in favor of promoting "humanity."

After all, the essence of being human and the definition of humanity should be determined by those awesome sections of our brain that have made us unique and special, not the small, primitive portion that we have in common with all other species.

We humans have proven beyond any doubt that we can cooperate and work together to overcome seemingly impossible obstacles. Surely the majority of us can make the choice to overcome some ancient, outdated instincts. With enough individual effort our entire planet could be transformed into a "Garden of Eden." It would be a long, hard struggle but what a reward! Even God might indulge in a feeling of pride.

www.ingramcontent.com/pod-product-compliance
Lightning Source LLC
Chambersburg PA
CBHW031246280526
45784CB00004B/1734